A Practical Guide to Library of Congress Subject Headings

A Practical Guide to Library of Congress Subject Headings

Karen Snow

ROWMAN & LITTLEFIELD
Lanham • Boulder • New York • London

Published by Rowman & Littlefield
An imprint of The Rowman & Littlefield Publishing Group, Inc.
4501 Forbes Boulevard, Suite 200, Lanham, Maryland 20706
www.rowman.com

6 Tinworth Street, London, SE11 5AL, United Kingdom

Copyright © 2021 by The Rowman & Littlefield Publishing Group, Inc.

All rights reserved. No part of this book may be reproduced in any form or by any electronic or mechanical means, including information storage and retrieval systems, without written permission from the publisher, except by a reviewer who may quote passages in a review.

British Library Cataloguing in Publication Information Available

Library of Congress Cataloging-in-Publication Data

Name: Snow, Karen, 1977–, author.
Title: A practical guide to Library of Congress subject headings / Karen Snow.
Description: Lanham : Rowman & Littlefield, [2021] | Includes bibliographical references and index. | Summary: "Here's a resource that uses language non-catalogers can understand and provides hands-on, user-friendly training in LCSH. The book offers a brief history of LCSH, discusses basic principles of subject analysis, explains the key principles of LCSH, and details how to choose and apply LCSH subject headings and subheadings"—Provided by publisher.
Identifiers: LCCN 2021000814 (print) | LCCN 2021000815 (ebook) | ISBN 9781538142998 (cloth) | ISBN 9781538143001 (paperback) | ISBN 9781538143018 (ebook)
Subjects: LCSH: Subject headings, Library of Congress. | Subject headings, Library of Congress—Problems, exercises, etc.
Classification: LCC Z695.Z8 S66 2021 (print) | LCC Z695.Z8 (ebook) | DDC 025.4/9—dc23
LC record available at https://lccn.loc.gov/2021000814
LC ebook record available at https://lccn.loc.gov/2021000815

Contents

Preface		vii
Acknowledgments		xi
1	Library of Congress Subject Headings in a Nutshell	1
2	Basic Principles of Subject Analysis	11
3	Searching and Browsing LCSH in Classification Web	19
4	Subdivisions and Free-Floating Subdivisions	29
5	MARC Coding of LCSH	37
6	The *Subject Headings Manual* (*SHM*)	49
7	Geographic Subject Headings and Subdivisions	59
8	Personal Name Subject Headings and Biographies	69
9	Fiction	81
10	Conclusion and LCSH Resources	101

Appendix A: Answers to End-of-Chapter Exercises 105

Appendix B: Form and Topical Free-Floating Subdivisions 127

Appendix C: Names of Places in Free-Floating Subdivisions 143

Appendix D: Names of Persons in Free-Floating Subdivisions 155

Glossary 163

Index 167

About the Author 169

Preface

The year 1898 is generally recognized as the date that the Library of Congress subject headings (LCSH) emerged as a distinct entity. Using the American Library Association's *List of Subject Headings for Use in Dictionary Catalogs* as a jumping-off point, the Library of Congress sought to build a list of terms that accurately represented the subject matter of its fast-growing collections. Over one hundred years later, the use of LCSH has expanded well beyond the Library of Congress into the catalogs of libraries all over the world. LCSH is a mainstay in a wide range of libraries and information centers. If you use one of these institution's catalogs, you will most likely encounter LCSH. For this reason, having at least a foundational knowledge of how to find and assign LCSH is helpful to effectively utilize the library catalog.

LCSH primarily contains terms that describe the subject matter of a resource—what the resource is *about*. It is a **controlled vocabulary**, which means, at the most basic level, that it is a standardized list of terms, or "headings," that is used to describe something. Controlled vocabularies are often, but not always, used to provide subject access to resources. One could have a standardized list of car models, languages, or candle fragrances. Ideally, controlled vocabulary terms are *unique* (only one heading represents a particular topic) and are applied *consistently* so that all works on a particular topic can be found under one term. For example, if you use LCSH, all resources in a collection that are generally about dogs should be assigned the LC subject heading *Dogs* and not *Dog* (singular) or *Canine*. If someone is trying to locate all items in a library collection that are about dogs, it would take extra time to search the different ways of referring to that animal. The use of a controlled vocabulary helps to cut down on this labor by choosing one "authorized" term that stands in for all of these different ways of expressing the same concept. In addition, it is common for controlled vocabularies to list nonauthorized variant forms alongside the authorized one so individuals searching under *Canine*, let's say, can still locate works on this topic without having to know beforehand what the authorized subject heading (*Dogs*) actually is.

Controlled vocabularies like LCSH help catalogers overcome common issues with language so that users can more efficiently locate and discover resources. These issues include the existence of synonymous concepts, as in my *Dogs* example above, but also homographs—words that have different meanings but are spelled the same. Examples of homographs include *bat* (animal and sports equipment), *patient* (willing to wait or someone receiving medical treatment), and *mercury* (the Roman deity, metallic element, planet, or car). Even though keyword searching of catalogs and databases is (and will likely continue to be) popular, the issues described above reveal the limits of keywords. You can certainly find *some* resources on dogs by performing a keyword search of *Canine* in a library catalog, but it will not provide as many relevant resources as a targeted subject search of *Dogs* in a catalog that consistently uses LCSH. Even if you prefer to use keyword searching by default, the inclusion of controlled vocabularies in library catalogs increases your chances of finding resources on that topic. According to one study by Tina Gross, Arlene Taylor, and Daniel Joudrey, almost 30 percent of catalog records would not appear in a search result list if controlled vocabulary terms were not included.[1] As you will see from reading this book, working with controlled vocabularies can be challenging, but they do improve catalog search results if applied correctly and consistently in catalog records.

Whether you are merely curious about LCSH or in desperate need of assistance figuring out the complex rules of LCSH for your work duties or homework assignment, I hope this book can help. As the title suggests, this is a practical guide to locating and assigning LCSH, so I will not delve too deeply into the more theoretical aspects of the standard. Nonetheless, there are principles of subject analysis in general, and for LCSH specifically, that are important to know in order to use LCSH effectively.

Therefore, I will provide a brief explanation of subject analysis in chapter 2 after I offer an overview of LCSH in chapter 1. I will also thread discussion of subject analysis throughout each subsequent chapter by referring to Library of Congress's instruction manual for LCSH, the *Subject Headings Manual* (*SHM*). I will do a deeper dive into the *SHM* in chapter 6.

In chapter 3 we will explore one of the main tools used to search and browse LCSH, Classification Web. The common use of subdivisions in LCSH can be a major source of confusion and frustration, so I devote the entirety of chapter 4 to this topic, but it will pop up in other chapters as well. Since the Machine-Readable Cataloging (MARC) standard is, as of this writing, the main encoding standard used in library catalogs, I will demonstrate how to encode LCSH using MARC starting in chapter 5. If you do not use MARC in your work or class, feel free to skip that chapter and subsequent mentions of it.

Chapter 7 will cover the use of geographic places as subject headings and subdivisions, and chapter 8 will guide you through finding and assigning personal name subject headings that are needed when describing biographical material, literary criticisms, and other resources that emphasize a person's life or works. Fiction works are incredibly popular, especially in public and school libraries, so I will cover the ins and outs of assigning LCSH to fiction in chapter 9. Finally, in the last chapter, I will summarize the resources I have used in this book and offer additional advice and resources that I think will be helpful if you want to explore LCSH further.

This book is the next phase of my passion project that began with the publication of *A Practical Guide to Library of Congress Classification*. In that text, as in this one, I explain a rather complicated cataloging standard in a straightforward way, with limited jargon, so that both newcomers and those well seasoned in LCSH can understand the basics and feel empowered to tackle the subject cataloging of whatever resource you encounter. I am also a firm believer in the need to balance theory with practice in cataloging. LCSH is much easier to grasp when you actually work with it as opposed to simply read about it. That is why I included practice exercises at the end of most chapters, with my answers at the end of the book, so you can self-assess your learning each step of the way. Ready? Let's get started!

NOTE

1. Tina Gross, Arlene G. Taylor, and Daniel N. Joudrey, "Still a Lot to Lose: The Role of Controlled Vocabulary in Keyword Searching," *Cataloging and Classification Quarterly* 53, no. 1 (2015): 1–39.

Acknowledgments

Tim Butzen-Cahill, your feedback and support throughout this entire project have been invaluable and are deeply appreciated. Your faith in this book means a great deal to me, and it is a stronger work because of you. Thank you!

Lauren Enjeti has once again come through on bringing my vision to life through her fantastic illustrations. You are amazing!

Thank you to Library of Congress for granting me permission to reproduce screen captures of *Classification Web* and the Library of Congress Authorities website. This is a much more accessible book because of your generosity.

To my students: thank you for making me a better teacher every day.

Finally, I could not do what I do without the steadfast support of friends and family. Robby and Eleanor: I love you—this one's for you.

1

Library of Congress Subject Headings in a Nutshell

The Library of Congress subject headings (LCSH) list is a controlled vocabulary that includes terms that primarily refer to the subject matter of a work. LCSH was developed in the late nineteenth and early twentieth centuries by the Library of Congress (LC) for use in its catalog. Over time, and mainly due to the proliferation of Library of Congress cards through the LC card distribution program, LCSH was adopted by other libraries within the United States and around the world. Even though the Library of Congress does take into consideration the wishes of other libraries in its maintenance of LCSH, the vocabulary is tailored largely to the resources that the Library of Congress collects, and the terminology and scope of the list reflect this. The Library of Congress serves many scholars and government officials, so you will notice that LCSH tends to include more scientific and legal terminology than found in popular language.

To a large extent, the Library of Congress uses what is called *literary warrant* to determine what terms to include in LCSH rather than a philosophical framework. **Literary warrant** means that published literature principally determines what subject headings are included in LCSH; if nothing has been published on a particular subject, it is less likely to be added to LCSH. For this reason, the subject headings included in LCSH are more of a mirror of the subject matter presented in published resources rather than an accurate representation of human knowledge.

In addition to this preference for terms used in published literature, LCSH contains language that reflects the biases of the creators of the system. One could easily write a book about bias in LCSH and subject vocabularies generally,[1] so I will not include a detailed discussion of this topic here. Nonetheless, it is important to understand that all cataloging standards, because they are created by human beings for specific purposes, are biased in their representation of the world (cultures, people, professions, ideas, etc.). For example, since the Library of Congress serves the United States government, US legal codes have an outsized influence on the terminology included in LCSH. That is why the Library of Congress continues to use the subject heading *Illegal aliens* (a US legal term that some people find offensive)[2] instead of the more commonly used term *undocumented immigrants*. For this reason, it is imperative to recognize that LCSH is not (and never has been) a perfect standard. It is a dynamic resource that is updated regularly, yet it is still flawed and therefore needs to be continually questioned and revised to more accurately represent resources in a way that does not solely reflect one group's point of view, as LCSH has done historically.

That said, let's return to the nuts and bolts (or, as LCSH would say, *Bolts and nuts*) of LCSH. When applying subject controlled vocabularies such as the LCSH, the cataloger's focus should be on what the work is *about* as opposed to what it *is*, but there will be exceptions to this rule, as we will see. LCSH mostly contains what are called **main headings**— terms that describe what a work is primarily about. In LCSH, main headings are mostly *topical*; in other words, they represent a concept, such as *Love* or *Sadness*, or objects, such as *Cats* or *Trees*. However, you will find the occasional geographic place, format, event, time period, or name (personal, family, etc.) in LCSH as well.

Main headings are not always single words, like *Dogs* or *Art*. They can also be compound nouns or complex phrases, for example. Here is a quick guide to the different forms main headings can take, and some examples of each, from the *Subject Headings Manual* (*SHM*) H 0180 (more about this resource in a moment):

Simple nouns: *Children*; *Dogs*; *Libraries*
Compound nouns: *Bioengineering*; *Electrometallurgy*
Nouns with parenthetical qualifiers: *Seals (Animals)*; *Crack (Drug)*
Nouns with adjectives: *Gifted children*; *Wild dogs*; *Academic libraries*; *Sculpture, American*; *Science, Ancient*

Phrases with prepositions: *Teachers of gifted children; Photography of dogs; Photocopying services in libraries*
Compound phrases: *Children and animals; Bolts and nuts; Comic books, strips, etc.*
Complex phrases: *Names carved on trees; Infants switched at birth; Monkeys as aids for people with disabilities*

LCSH also contains **subdivisions**, terms that add further specificity to main headings, such as a time period, geographic place, or other topics, if needed. A hyphen, either long (–) or short (-), indicates a heading/subdivision relationship in LCSH. For example, LCSH contains the main heading *Dogs* that should be assigned to works that are primarily about dogs. LCSH also contains *Dogs–Housing*, a main heading and subdivision combination that should be assigned to works that are primarily about housing dogs. I will cover subdivisions in more depth in chapter 4.

LCSH contains many types of relationships among terms that can be found in controlled vocabularies generally, such as equivalence relationships, hierarchical relationships, and associative relationships. These are important concepts, so I will discuss each one and provide examples.

Equivalence relationships occur when a preferred or authorized term is chosen to represent a concept and is connected to nonauthorized variant terms that are considered synonymous within the context of the controlled vocabulary. For example, the LCSH *Dwellings* (the authorized term) has an equivalence relationship to nonauthorized variant terms *Domiciles, Homes,* and *Houses*. The relationship is reciprocal (works both ways) so that each of the nonauthorized variant terms are connected to the authorized term. The entry for *Houses* in LCSH, for example, will prompt you to use *Dwellings* instead.

Figure 1.1. Dog housing. *Lauren Enjeti.*

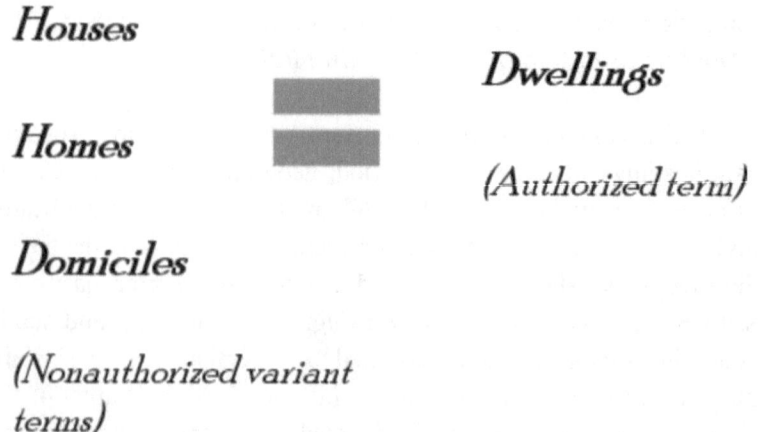

Figure 1.2. Equivalence relationships. *Karen Snow.*

Hierarchical relationships arrange terms according to where the creator of the vocabulary believes the terms fit in a broader and narrower context. Sometimes these hierarchical relationships are "whole-part"—the narrower concepts represent objects that are often quite literally parts of a broader object. The LCSH entry for *Books*, for instance, lists narrower terms *Colophons* and *Title pages*, both parts of a book. Membership within a particular class constitutes another hierarchical relationship where "types" or "kinds" of the broader term are made into narrower terms. For example, within LCSH, *Bathrooms*, *Bedrooms*, and *Dining rooms* are all narrower terms for *Rooms* because they are all types of rooms. "Instance" relationships are another type of hierarchical relationship that occurs when a narrower term is considered an example of the broader term. *Monopoly (Game)* and *Scrabble (Game)*, both types of board games, are narrower terms under *Board games* in LCSH, for example.

Finally, **associative relationships** arise when a concept is similar to, but does not have an equivalence or hierarchical relationship with, a related concept. For example, *Bibliography*, *Cataloging*, and *International Standard Book Numbers* are related to *Books*, according to LCSH, but are not synonymous with books or broader/narrower terms for books.

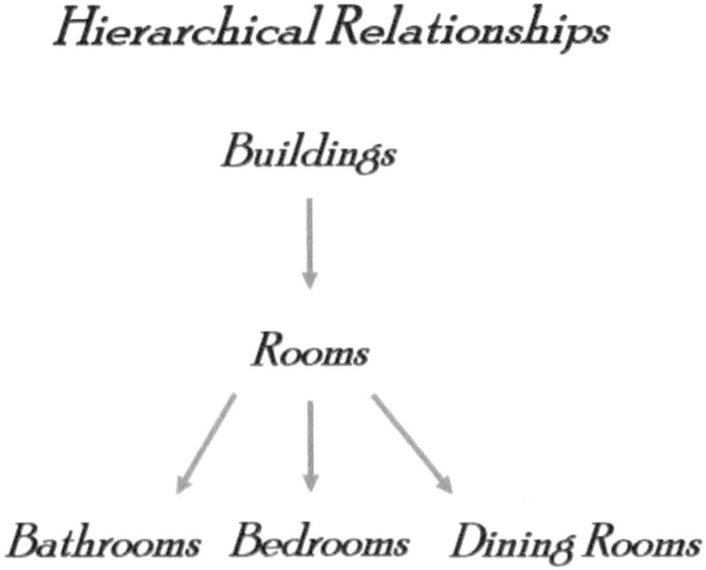

Hierarchical Relationships

Buildings
↓
Rooms
↙ ↓ ↘
Bathrooms   Bedrooms   Dining Rooms

Figure 1.3.   Hierarchical relationships. *Karen Snow*.

Associative Relationships

Books   ≠   Bibliography

           Cataloging

Related but not equivalent

           International Standard Book Numbers

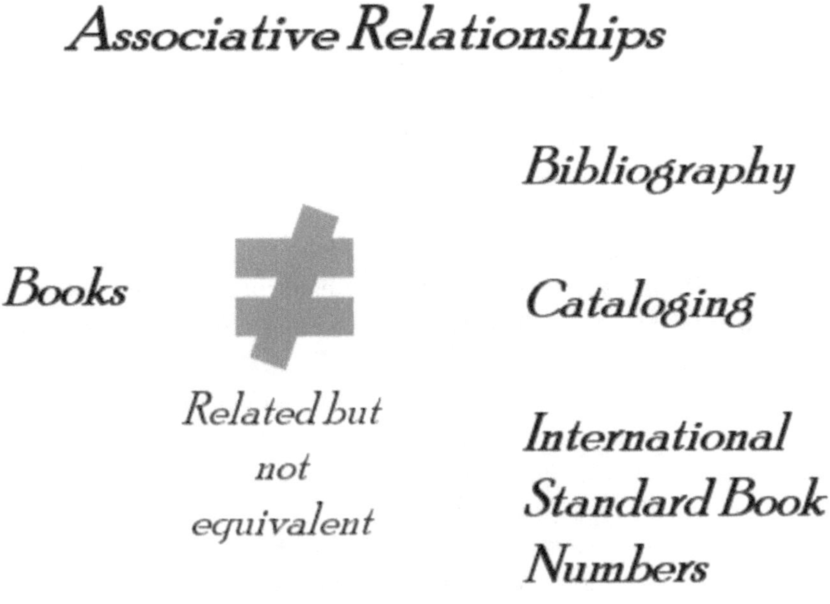

Figure 1.4.   Associative relationships. *Karen Snow*.

Associative relationships are not included for every entry in LCSH, but they can be helpful when they are.

In addition to understanding the different types of relationships you will encounter in LCSH, it is important to understand other concepts, such as specificity and scope matching, to determine which terms are appropriate to assign to a resource. When assigning LCSH to a resource, or searching for LCSH in a catalog, Library of Congress wants you to be as specific as possible. The concept of *specificity* is very important in LCSH and can be found in other controlled vocabularies as well. It is covered in the *Subject Headings Manual* H 0180. **Specificity** can be defined in two primary ways: (1) it refers to how closely the topic of a resource matches the term(s) applied, and (2) it refers to the lowest part of a hierarchy within a particular context.

Take a look at this hierarchy of topics moving from a broad topic (*Animals*) to a more specific topic (*German shepherd dog*):

Animals
    Domestic animals
        Animal breeds
            Dog breeds
                German shepherd dog

Within the context of this hierarchy, *German shepherd dog* is the most specific entry. If I need to assign a subject heading to a book about dog breeds generally, *Dog breeds* would be the most appropriate—the most *specific* term—for that book even though it is not the most specific term in the context of the above hierarchy. *German shepherd dog* would be too specific for a book on dog breeds generally because the book is not just about German shepherd dogs. On the other hand, if the book was indeed about German shepherd dogs, then *German shepherd dog* would be appropriate to assign to that book.

The concept of specificity is tied to the principle of *scope-match* coverage, another important concept in LCSH. **Scope-match** "refers to the level of depth at which books are indexed."[3] In addition, Library of Congress notes about scope-match that

> as a rule, catalogers try to assign only as many headings to a work as are necessary to sum up the subject of the work as a whole. In other words, they

will not usually assign headings for each individual chapter or section of a book. The result is that most catalog records receive from two to five headings rather than ten or fifteen, and many books receive fewer than three.[4]

The principle of scope-match explains why a cataloger using LCSH will not assign subject headings for every dog breed (German shepherds, collies, poodles, etc.) to a general book on dog breeds. You should focus on the topic of the book as a whole as opposed to teasing out the parts.

Since Library of Congress cataloging practice frequently becomes common cataloging practice in the library world, I will note two rules of thumb that Library of Congress catalogers *must* follow and that you can *choose* to follow if you prefer (but sometimes local policy dictates that you should). One is the "20 percent rule," which states that you should assign a subject heading only if 20 percent or more of the resource covers the topic (*Subject Headings Manual* H 0180). For example, it is fine to assign a subject heading for *Apples* to a book about fruit if the author devotes 50 percent of the work to apples and the rest to other fruits, but you would not assign *Apples* to a fruit encyclopedia that discusses all fruits equally. Another rule of thumb is to assign as many subject headings as you believe are appropriate to capture the main subject matter of a resource (following the above guidance, of course), but do not assign more than ten subject headings (*Subject Headings Manual* H 0180). These two rules of thumb are helpful when you are cataloging a complex or multitopic resource and need to stay focused on the most relevant subject headings.

Now that we have the basics down, let's talk about how to actually find LCSH. The LCSH list can be found in multiple places on the web (it is no longer published in print). In this book, I will use primarily a subscription-based tool called Classification Web (https://classweb.org/) to provide examples. Classification Web also contains other Library of Congress standards, such as the LC Children's Subject Headings, which is useful for describing fiction and nonfiction works in public and school libraries (I will talk more about this resource in chapter 9, "Fiction"), and the Library of Congress Genre/Form Terms for Library and Archival Materials, which contains terms for various forms and genres (more about form and genre in the next chapter and in chapter 9).

If you do not have access to Classification Web, there are other resources on the web that provide access to LCSH free of charge. One of these resources is the set of PDFs provided by the Library of Congress on their website (https://www.loc.gov/aba/cataloging/subject/). It does not have the enhanced functionality of Classification Web, but it is freely accessible.

You can also find LCSH in what are called authority records using the Library of Congress's Authorities website (http://authorities.loc.gov/), through the Library of Congress's linked data service (http://id.loc.gov/), or through an OCLC product such as Connexion (if your institution has a subscription). Authority records, which I will discuss in more depth in later chapters, can be more useful than Classification Web as they often include additional background information about a subject heading. Therefore, I encourage you to explore multiple sources of LCSH when assigning headings and subdivisions.

The Library of Congress's *Subject Headings Manual* (*SHM*) is the source of much of the content in this and subsequent chapters. The *SHM* is Library of Congress's instruction manual for creating and assigning LCSH. I will refer to it throughout the book and explore some of the guidance in more depth in chapter 6. Whenever you see *SHM* H[insert number here], know that I am referring to a specific instruction sheet in the *Subject Headings Manual*. You can access the *SHM* through Cataloger's Desktop if your institution subscribes to it, or you can access *SHM* free of charge from this web page: https://www.loc.gov/aba/publications/FreeSHM/freeshm.html.

In the next chapter, I will cover the basics of subject analysis, a notoriously fascinating yet challenging process in many cases. I will describe a method (SLAM) that I hope will make the subject analysis process a little easier to absorb. Before you move on, why don't you stay a while longer and work on some exercises to test your knowledge of this chapter?

EXERCISES

Using the information in this chapter, answer the following questions and compare your responses to the answers provided at the end of this book.

1. What does the Library of Congress primarily rely on to determine which terms should be included in LCSH?
2. Name two places on the web where you can find LCSH.
3. Read each explanation below, and identify the type of relationship described as an equivalence relationship, a hierarchical relationship, or an associative relationship.
    a. In LCSH, *Solar system* is a narrower term under *Milky Way* but is broader than *Planets*. What type of relationship do these terms have?
    b. *Buckets* and *pails* are considered synonyms in LCSH. What type of relationship do these terms have?
    c. The LCSH *Folklore* has several related terms, such as *Mythology* and *Storytelling*, that do not have the same meaning and are not considered broader or narrower terms. What type of relationship do these terms have?
4. Using the principle of specificity and the LCSH hierarchy (economics → economic policy → government spending policy → employment subsidies), answer the following questions:
    a. Is it appropriate to assign *Economics* to a general work on economic policy? Explain.
    b. Is it appropriate to assign *Employment subsidies* to a general work on government spending policy that discusses employment subsidies among other government spending policies? Explain.
    c. Is it appropriate to assign *Economic policy* to a general work on economic policy? Explain.
5. Use the principle of scope-match and the above *Economics* hierarchy to determine which response (assign the headings for each type of policy or assign the general topic heading *Economic policy*) is the most appropriate to the scenarios provided in a and b. Explain your choice.
    a. A work on economic policy comprised of three equal parts that cover government spending policy, labor policy, and monetary policy (all types of economic policy)
    b. A work on economic policy with twelve chapters, each covering a different type of policy

NOTES

1. In fact, many people *have* written books on this topic. I recommend the following: Melissa Adler, *Cruising the Library: Perversities in the Organization of Knowledge* (New York: Fordham University Press, 2017); Sanford Berman, *Prejudices and Antipathies: A Tract on the LC Subject Heads Concerning People*, 1993 ed. (Jefferson, NC: McFarland, 1993), http://www.sanfordberman.org/prejant.htm; Hope Olson, *The Power to Name: Locating the Limits of Subject Representation in Libraries* (Norwell, MA: Kluwer Academic, 2002).

2. See Jasmine Aguilera, "Another Word for 'Illegal Alien' at the Library of Congress: Contentious," *New York Times*, July 22, 2016, https://nyti.ms/2k4EsRf.

3. Library of Congress, "Doing Research at the Library of Congress: Three Basic Principles of Library of Congress Subject Headings," last modified December 1, 2016, https://www.loc.gov/rr/main/research/scopematch.html.

4. Library of Congress, "Doing Research at the Library of Congress: Three Basic Principles of Library of Congress Subject Headings."

2

Basic Principles of Subject Analysis

Imagine a table in front of you with the following items: a duck puppet used for a children's puppet show, a DVD of the dystopian science-fiction film *The Matrix*, and a picture book for children that features a school for crayons. If you were asked what each of these items was *about*, you would likely have difficulty answering that question, but for different reasons (assuming you are even familiar with these resources to begin with!).

Is a duck puppet *about* anything?

Sure, *The Matrix* is *about* artificial intelligence and computer hackers, but what about its genre: dystopian science fiction? Isn't that important as well?

The children's picture book is obvious enough, right? It's about crayons! But wait—while browsing through the book, you notice that the main crayon, named Red, despite the clearly labeled red wrapper surrounding him, can only produce the color blue. It takes an insightful crayon colleague to point out that Red the crayon is, in fact, Red the *blue* crayon after all. Is this book still *just* about crayons?

Figure 2.1. What are you about, duck puppet? *Lauren Enjeti.*

I have taken you through this strange exercise to demonstrate the complexity of subject analysis. **Subject analysis** is the process of determining what a resource is about and, to a lesser degree, its form and/or genre. This process is sometimes referred to as determining *aboutness*, in contrast to determining *is-ness* (the first resource mentioned above *is* a duck puppet as opposed to *about* a duck puppet, for example), but as my definition of subject analysis demonstrates, is-ness may play a role as well. The subject terminology we use frequently contains "form" aspects that emphasize physical characteristics and what the resource *is* and "genre" aspects that emphasize themes in the intellectual content of a resource, such as technique or style. Form examples include dictionaries, diaries, and maps. Genre examples include detective and mystery fiction, war films, and rock and roll music. Resources can be described in terms of both aboutness and is-ness.[1] For example, *The Diary of a Young Girl* by Anne Frank is *about* Anne Frank and her family during the two years they spent hiding from Nazis in the Netherlands during World War II (aboutness), and it is a diary (form) and a memoir (genre). I will delve into form and genre on occasion in this book, but the primary focus will be on determining the *aboutness* of a resource and then assigning subject terminology accordingly.

In library and information science literature, the determination of aboutness and form/genre is often called *conceptual analysis*, and converting the ideas produced through the process of conceptual analysis into controlled vocabulary terms is called *translation*.[2] Both conceptual analysis and translation are usually part of the subject analysis process and can be challenging in their own ways. One major impediment when analyzing the subject of a resource is that those who assign subject terms frequently do not have intimate knowledge of the resource, whether it is a book, a movie, a video game, or an adorable children's puppet. And even if you *have* read the book or watched the film, determining what it is *about* (conceptual analysis) and then converting that into a controlled vocabulary term (translation) is still tricky. For this reason, I recommend Library of Congress's SLAM method to guide you through the subject analysis process.[3] SLAM stands for **S**can, **L**ook for, **A**sk yourself, and **M**entally compose. Let's look at each step of this method:

Scan: The first step of the SLAM method is to scan the parts of a resource that provide the most clues about its subject focus. Which areas you examine depends on the resource, of course (films do not have title pages, for example), but here are some standard places to start:

- title page (or title screen, card, etc.)
- introduction
- preface
- table of contents
- front and back cover/dust jacket (or front and back of the container)
- bibliography and index
- any other documentation that is on or comes with the resource (like an affixed label or instruction sheet)

In addition, some books have what is called Library of Congress Cataloging-in-Publication (CIP) data: prepublication information about the book most often printed on the back side of the title page (called the "title page verso"). If present, the CIP frequently contains helpful information about the subject matter of the work. It may contain a summary as well as the subject terms the Library of Congress (or partnering institutions) has assigned to the book. For example, the book *Ruth Bader Ginsburg: My Own Words* contains the following Library of Congress subject headings (LCSH) strings in the CIP:

Ginsburg, Ruth Bader
Women judges–United States–Biography
Women lawyers–United States–Biography
United States. Supreme Court–Biography

It is becoming more common for juvenile fiction books to include a summary in the CIP as well as subject terms from the Library of Congress Children's Subject Headings, a list I will discuss in chapter 9, "Fiction." The information in the CIP may be enough to describe the resource in hand, or it may be a good starting point—consider assigning additional terms if time and institutional policy allow for it.

Look for: The next step is to identify keywords or phrases in the above sources that are particularly helpful at conveying what the resource is *about*. For example, the title of the book *A History of American Higher Education* pretty clearly states that the book is about the history of

American higher education, but even if the title is misleading or unhelpful, you can usually find keywords in other parts of the resource that give more detail on what it is about. A few other aspects to consider:

- author's intent (e.g., Did the author intend the resource to be fiction or nonfiction?)
- intended audience (e.g., Is the resource aimed at children or adults?)
- special viewpoint (e.g., Is the resource geared toward the general public or those with more specialized knowledge?)

Also identify the resource's form or genre if that aspect stands out. For instance, is the resource a dictionary? Is it fiction or nonfiction? If the resource is a music album, is there any indication of the musical genre or style? You may need to look at sources beyond the resource itself, such as the publisher's website, to answer some of these questions because subject, form, and genre information may not always be obvious.

Ask yourself: Once you have scanned the resource and looked for keywords or phrases, you should ask yourself, What is this resource about? There may not be a single answer to this question, so you will likely need to ask additional questions, such as:

- Are there multiple topics covered or just one?
- If there are multiple topics, what is their relationship to one another? Is one topic discussed more frequently than others?
- Is a time period, geographic place, or person emphasized?

The answers to these questions should provide further information about the subject matter of the resource and keywords you can use in the last step of the SLAM method.

Mentally compose: The final part of the SLAM method is to mentally compose a statement about the resource using the information you have collected in the first three steps. Begin the statement with "This resource is about" or similar wording. Composing such a statement can help you focus your attention on topics that you will need to find in a controlled vocabulary, such as the Library of Congress subject headings. Here are some examples of "mentally composed" statements:

Basic Principles of Subject Analysis   15

> This resource is about Library of Congress subject headings.
>
> This picture book for children is about a fictional crayon that is confused about his identity.
>
> This dystopian science-fiction film is about computer hackers who discover that the world is not as it seems and fight against an artificial intelligence that has enslaved humans.
>
> This encyclopedia is about different styles of houses throughout history and is geared toward real estate agents.
>
> This book is about the history of higher education in the United States, specifically in the nineteenth and twentieth centuries.

Once you have completed the SLAM method, hopefully you will have enough information about the resource to complete the *translation* part of subject analysis and find appropriate terms in whatever controlled vocabulary you are using. However, keep in mind that the words you use in your statement may not match up perfectly to controlled vocabulary terms. For example, the LCSH for Library of Congress subject headings is *Subject headings, Library of Congress* and the LCSH for houses is *Dwellings*. Try different search strategies and synonyms to locate the appropriate term (assuming there is one to be found).

Let's discuss some additional areas of potential confusion for those new to assigning subject terminology. One area of confusion is the number of subject terms you should assign and, if you need to assign multiple terms, how to determine if they should stay together in one field or be separated into different fields. As for how many subject terms to assign, remember that the Library of Congress does have special instructions for its catalogers on this topic (do not assign more than ten subject headings to one resource), but as a general rule of thumb, you should assign as many terms as needed to cover the main topics of the resource. What to do if you need multiple terms to describe a resource, and whether you keep them together in one string of terms or separate them, depends on a few things.

First, a single term or string of terms may be sufficient to represent a multifaceted topic. For example, in LCSH, the topic of the history of American higher education can be expressed in one string of terms:

Education, Higher–United States–History

A subject heading string can contain multiple topics or forms as long as you follow the rules associated with the controlled vocabulary. In LCSH, for instance, you cannot simply include any term you want in the string. We will discuss this in more depth in chapter 4, "Subdivisions and Free-Floating Subdivisions." Therefore, if one term or string of terms cannot capture multiple distinct topics, you will most likely need to use multiple terms or multiple strings of terms. Resources with more complex themes will likely require the latter since it is important to keep ideas separate for easier retrieval. For example, a picture book for children that is about a fictional crayon with identity confusion is about a crayon but also identity, two very distinct concepts. Unless there is a controlled vocabulary that has a single term for the topic "crayon identity" (very unlikely, but it would be fascinating if that existed!), we will need to include both topics but use separate terms or strings of terms to represent those topics. This way, those looking for a children's book featuring crayons can find it just as easily as those looking for a children's book about identity who may not care if that message is conveyed using crayons, humans, or whatever. In LCSH, we would assign the following subject heading strings to the aforementioned book:

Crayons–Juvenile fiction
Identity (Psychology)–Juvenile fiction

This discussion naturally leads us to the subject analysis concepts of *precoordination* and *postcoordination*. According to Lois Mai Chan and Athena Salaba, these terms "refer to 'when' single-concept terms are combined to form complex subjects."[4]

Precoordination occurs when terms are combined within the controlled vocabulary itself or by someone assigning the vocabulary term(s) to create a complex topic. In other words, precoordinated terms representing a topic are determined prior to a user's search of a system.

Postcoordination, on the other hand, occurs when terms are combined by those searching the system. Even if there are precoordinated terms present in the system, postcoordinated searching will continue to be very common since users may not know what the precoordinated terms are. For instance, a user could perform a keyword search for "crayons," "identity," and "juvenile fiction" and still be able to find the crayon identity book.

No system will rely only on precoordination because there is no controlled vocabulary that is able to capture all complex topics in one term or one string of terms, as I mentioned previously. Precoordination is helpful nonetheless for bringing together topics that are specifically related to the resource in hand for a more efficient search, especially in current library systems. For example, if I am looking for a book on the history of American higher education, a more targeted approach would be to conduct a search for the precoordinated subject heading string *Education, Higher–United States–History*. A postcoordinated search for "higher education," "United States," and "history" would likely produce a long list of search results that will include works on each of these topics more generally. As library systems evolve, perhaps postcoordinated searches using *facets* (distinct and clearly defined categories) will become easier. Regardless, a certain amount of postcoordinated searching will always be necessary, as demonstrated by the "crayon identity" example above.

In this chapter, I covered the basics of subject analysis. It is far from a comprehensive treatment, but I hope that it provides a helpful foundation on which to build your LCSH knowledge. It is one thing to know how to find and assign subject headings; it's quite another to understand how to determine aboutness in the first place. The SLAM method is a solid framework that should help you more easily conceptualize the subject analysis process, regardless of what controlled vocabulary you use. After completing the end-of-chapter exercises below, place SLAM in your shiny new cataloging tool box, and let's move on to learning more about how to search and browse LCSH in Classification Web as well as demystify entries in LCSH (I am looking at you BT, SA, RT, UF, and NT!).

EXERCISES

Answer the following questions using information within this chapter.

1. What does SLAM stand for? What does SLAM help you do?
2. Name two sources of information that you should consult during the first step of the SLAM method.

3. What aspects of a resource should you consider beyond those examined in the first step of the SLAM method when identifying keywords or phrases that describe what the work is about?
4. What two actions typically occur during the subject analysis process, according to library and information science literature?
5. What is it called when single-concept terms are combined to form complex subjects *prior* to the user's search of a system?
6. Besides aboutness, what else might be important to identify in the subject analysis process?

NOTES

1. There is also *of-ness*, a concept that is particularly useful when describing what is depicted in visual resources, such as paintings and photographs.

2. Daniel N. Joudrey, Arlene G. Taylor, and David Miller, *Introduction to Cataloging and Classification*, 11th ed. (Santa Barbara, CA: Libraries Unlimited, 2015).

3. ALCTS/SAC-PCC/SCT Joint Initiative on Subject Training Materials, "Basic Subject Cataloging Using LCSH: Trainee's Manual," last modified July 2009, https://www.loc.gov/catworkshop/courses/basicsubject/pdf/lcsh-trnee-manual.pdf.

4. Lois Mai Chan and Athena Salaba, *Cataloging and Classification: An Introduction*, 4th ed. (Lanham, MD: Rowman & Littlefield, 2016), 477.

3

Searching and Browsing LCSH in Classification Web

Classification Web (https://classweb.org/) is a subscription-based tool from the Library of Congress Cataloging Distribution Service that contains multiple cataloging standards. It contains not only the Library of Congress subject headings (LCSH) but also the Library of Congress (LC) classification schedules, the Library of Congress children's subject headings, and the Library of Congress genre/form headings. To access Classification Web, go to https://classweb.org/. You will see the screen shown in figure 3.1. Click on the "ClassWeb Main Menu" option, and you will see the screen in figure 3.2.

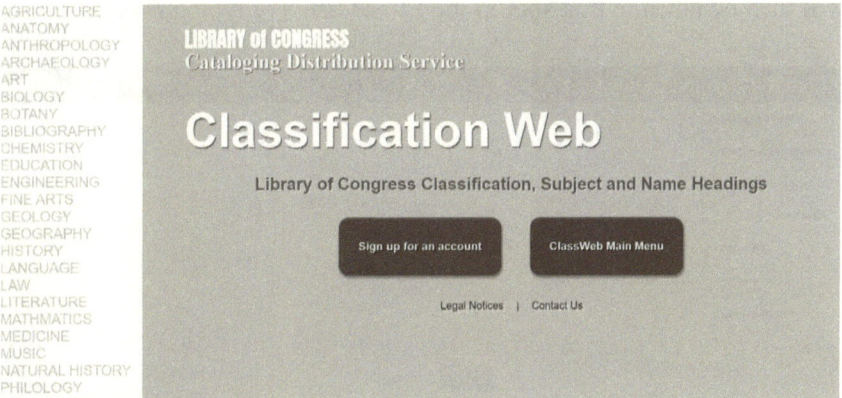

Figure 3.1. Classification Web homepage. *Library of Congress.*

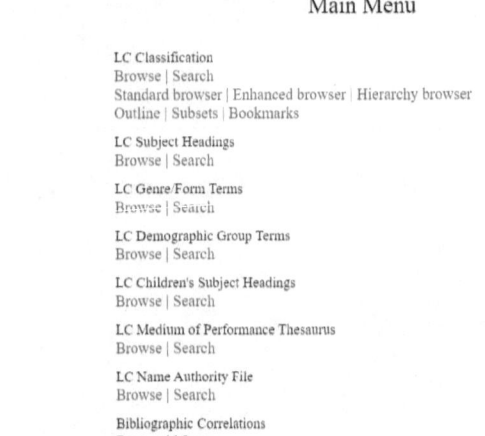

Figure 3.2. Classification Web main menu. *Library of Congress.*

Click on "Search" underneath "LC Subject Headings," and you will see a screen that prompts you for your username and password. You can also browse LCSH, but we will start by learning how to search. After you log on to Classification Web, you will see (among other things) the search options in figure 3.3. Note how each search label (such as "Subject heading" and "Free-floating subdiv") is hyperlinked. You can click on the label to find out more about each type of search. If you want to search for a Library of Congress subject heading, type the term into the first search box and click on "Search" at the bottom of the screen or hit Enter. You will then be taken to that spot in the LCSH list. Try typing *Fire power* in

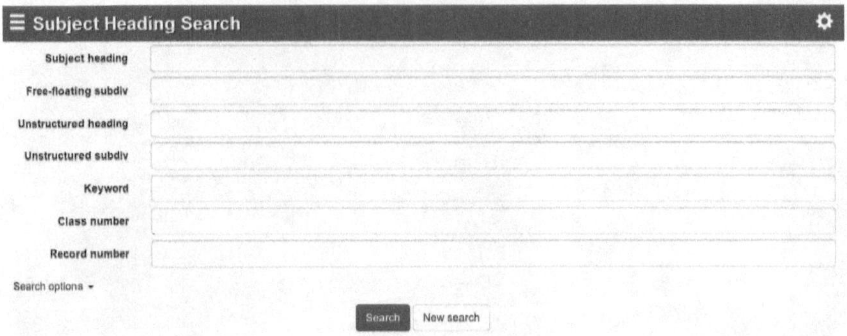

Figure 3.3. Subject heading search. *Library of Congress.*

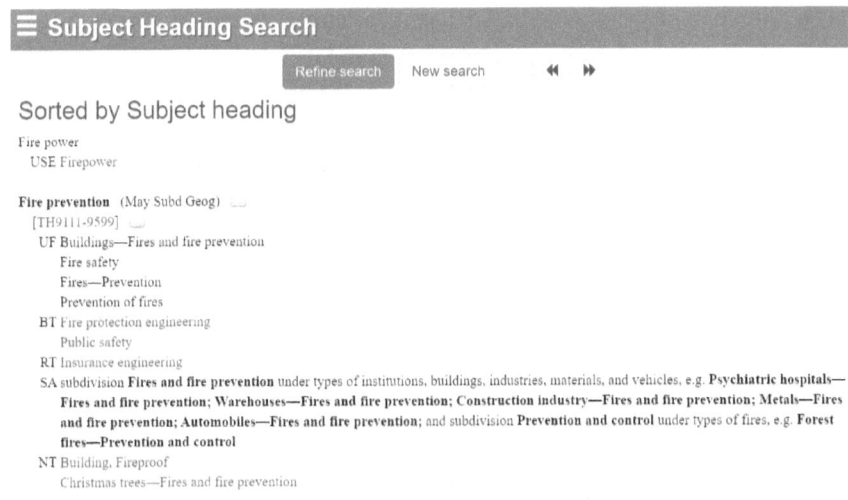

Figure 3.4. *Fire power* and *Fire prevention* entries. **Library of Congress.**

the Subject Heading search box. The results of that search are shown in figure 3.4.

Valid LC subject headings and subdivisions are in bold (e.g., *Fire prevention*) or hyperlinked (e.g., *Fire protection engineering*). Clicking

Table 3.1 Meaning of LCSH Codes

Code	Meaning	Definition
BT	Broader Term	A term that indicates the class, whole, or general topic to which the heading belongs. **Example:** *Domestic animals* is a BT for *Dogs*.
NT	Narrower Term	A term that indicates a specific class member, part, or instance of the heading to which it relates. **Example:** *Dogs* is a NT for *Domestic animals*.
RT	Related Term	A term or topic that is similar to, but does not have a hierarchical relationship with, the heading to which it relates. **Example:** *Feral animals* is a RT for *Domestic animals*.
SA	See Also	Heading or subdivision suggestions related to the selected term that may be useful to consider. **Example:** Individual animals, such as *Cats* and *Dogs*, are SAs under *Pets*.
UF	Used For	Terms that largely have the same meaning as the valid heading but should not be used. **Example:** *Domesticated animals* is a UF of *Domestic animals*.
USE	Use	Supplies valid heading or subdivision. **Example:** *Domestic animals* is the USE for *Domesticated animals*.

on the hyperlinked names will take you to those headings within LCSH. Invalid headings and subdivisions are in regular font (e.g., *Fire power*).

As I mentioned previously, LCSH is a hierarchical scheme that arranges terms according to where the Library of Congress believes they fit in a broader and narrower context. Therefore, you will see codes that designate broader (BT) and narrower (NT) terms. In addition, there are associative relationships (RT-related terms), cross-references to terms you should or should not use (used for and use), and suggestions for other headings or subdivisions that might also be useful (SA—see also). Table 3.1 explains the meaning behind the codes that you see throughout LCSH. The [term]–[term] indicates a heading–subdivision relationship, such as *Christmas trees–Fires and fire prevention*, which is a NT under *Fire prevention*. Not all subdivisions that can be used after a main heading will be listed in LCSH. Many are listed in the Free-Floating Subdivisions list, which I will discuss in the next chapter.

The identifier [TH9111-9599] immediately underneath *Fire prevention* is the range of Library of Congress classification (LCC) numbers that are associated with this topic. If you click on the hyperlink, it will take you directly to that entry within the LCC schedules in Classification Web.

The notation *(May Subd Geog)* to the right of *Fire prevention* is LC's way of stating that a subject heading or subdivision can have a geographic subdivision immediately following it. I will provide more details about geographic subdivision in chapter 4, "Subdivisions and Free-Floating

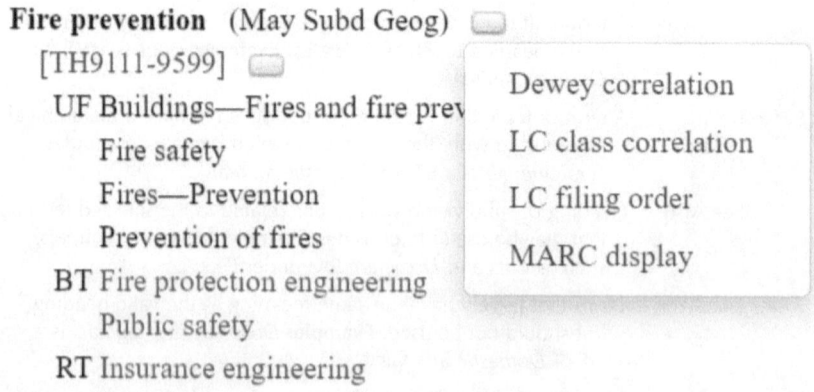

Figure 3.5. *Fire prevention* in Classification Web. *Library of Congress.*

Subdivisions" and chapter 7, "Geographic Subject Headings and Subdivisions."

If you click on the light-gray rectangle (I like to call it the "ghost rectangle") to the right of *(May Subd Geog)*, you will see a drop-down menu of options that can be changed by an account administrator within the Account settings. My menu contains these options: Dewey correlation, LC class correlation, LC filing order, and MARC display. See figure 3.5.

The Dewey and LC class correlation options provide class numbers from each of these classification systems that have been assigned to resources in the Library of Congress's collection with the same subject heading. For example, if I click on the LC class correlation option under *Fire prevention*'s ghost rectangle, as of this writing ten Library of Congress classification numbers have been assigned to resources that have *Fire prevention* as the subject heading (shown in figure 3.6).

The first class number listed is the one that is associated most often with the subject heading. The number in parentheses next to the class number

Fire prevention [Topical]
TH9145 (57)
TH9241 (15)
TH9146 (14)
TH9148 (8)
TH9111 (5)
TH9120 (4)
HG9715 (3)
S21 (2)
TH9115 (2)
TH9150 (2)

Figure 3.6. *Fire prevention in bibliographic correlations. Library of Congress.*

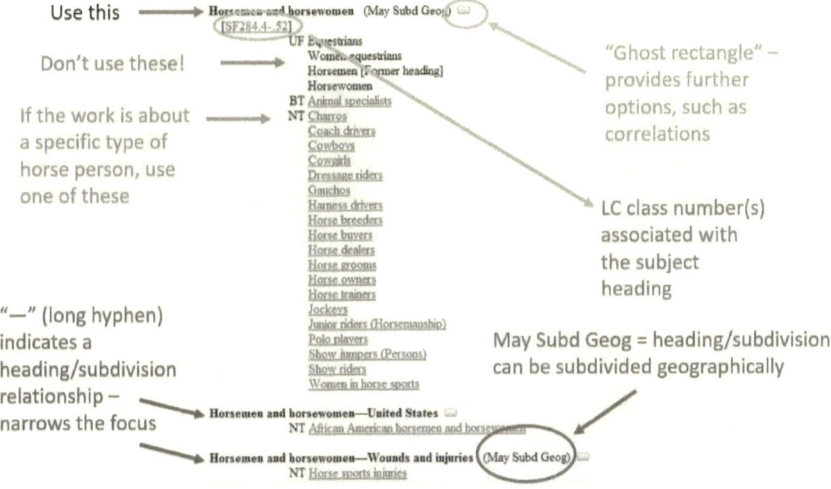

Figure 3.7. *Horsemen and Horsewomen entry explained. Library of Congress.*

Refine search
New search

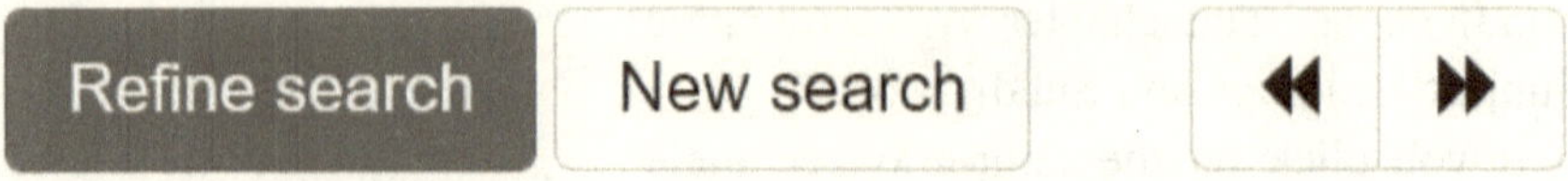

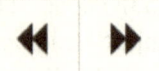

Figure 3.8. Classification Web navigation buttons. ***Library of Congress.***

indicates how many records in LC's catalog contain both that specific class number and the subject heading in the record. As of this writing, TH9145 and *Fire prevention* are paired in fifty-seven Library of Congress

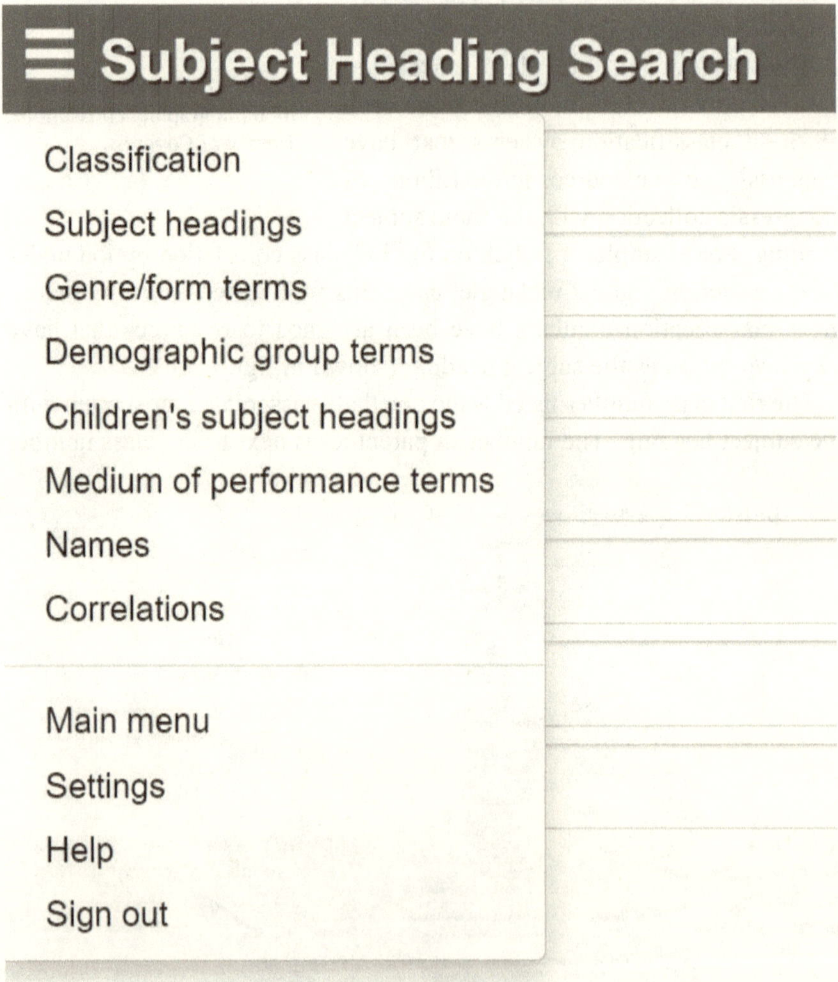
Subject Heading Search
Classification
Subject headings
Genre/form terms
Demographic group terms
Children's subject headings
Medium of performance terms
Names
Correlations
Main menu
Settings
Help
Sign out

Figure 3.9. Drop-down menu in Classification Web. ***Library of Congress.***

records. The numbers you see may be different from what you see here. LC filing order places LCSH entries in the order in which LC files them. Finally, if you choose MARC display, you will see the Machine-Readable Cataloging (MARC) authority record for that subject heading.

Figure 3.7 highlights the meaning of what you see in a typical LCSH entry in Classification Web. Please take note of the navigation buttons at the top of your screen, shown in figure 3.8. "Refine search" will take you back to the main LCSH search screen and retain your initial search terms.

"New search" will also take you back to the main LCSH search screen, but it will remove search terms used previously. The arrows have the following meanings:

<<   takes you back one full page in LCSH
\>>   takes you forward one full page in LCSH

Clicking on the three horizontal bars in the upper left-hand corner of the screen will reveal a drop-down menu with the options shown in figure 3.9. You can choose to go to one of the other resources in Classification Web (the top eight options in the menu), or you can choose "Main Menu" to go back to the main menu. When you are done using Classification Web, it is best to click on "Sign out." However, before we do, a quick note about "browsing" LCSH.

If you go back to the main menu of Classification Web and choose "Browse" underneath "LC Subject Headings," you will see a screen like figure 3.10. When you start typing a term, the helpful list of options in figure 3.11 appears.

Browsing LCSH is not that different from searching LCSH, but it does have the benefit of showing you options for LCSH and subdivisions as you type. You should receive the same results as an LCSH search. Use the drop-down menu to the right of the search magnifying glass to select

Figure 3.10.   Subject heading browse. *Library of Congress.*

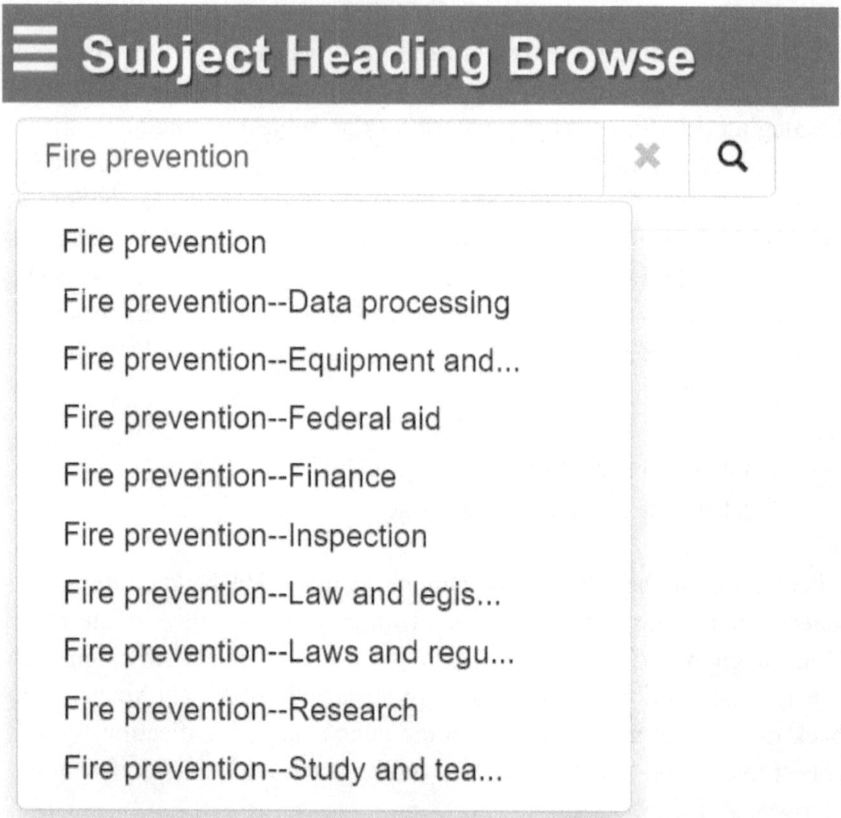

Subject Heading Browse

Fire prevention

- Fire prevention
- Fire prevention--Data processing
- Fire prevention--Equipment and...
- Fire prevention--Federal aid
- Fire prevention--Finance
- Fire prevention--Inspection
- Fire prevention--Law and legis...
- Fire prevention--Laws and regu...
- Fire prevention--Research
- Fire prevention--Study and tea...

Figure 3.11. Browsing *Fire prevention*. *Library of Congress*.

what you want to browse (LCSH, the Free-Floating Subdivisions list, a class number, etc).

This chapter provided guidance on how to navigate Classification Web to find Library of Congress main subject headings as well as information on how to understand the entries in LCSH. The next chapter will explore an important feature of LCSH: subdivisions.

EXERCISES

Use Classification Web (or another source for finding LCSH if you cannot access Classification Web) to answer the following questions.

1. What is the LCSH for book owners?
2. What is the LCSH for prehistoric animals?
3. What is the LCSH for boats?
4. What is the LCSH for futility?
5. What is the BT (broader term) associated with the LCSH *Unicorns*?
6. What is the RT (related term) associated with the LCSH *Fortune-telling by cards*?
7. What are the NTs (narrower terms) associated with *Imaginary vehicles*?
8. What are the UF (used for) headings associated with *Alchemy*?
9. What does the SA (see also) note say at LCSH *Clothing and dress*?
10. Can the LCSH *Desserts* be subdivided geographically? What about the LCSH *Desserts in art*?

4

Subdivisions and Free-Floating Subdivisions

Subdivisions are an important yet complex feature of Library of Congress subject headings (LCSH) that allows you to extend the main subject heading for greater specificity. In fact, when subdivisions are present, it is considered a **subject heading string**—one main subject heading and one or more subdivisions. According to the *Subject Headings Manual* (*SHM*) H 1075—Subdivisions, there are four types of subdivision in LCSH (see figures 4.1 through 4.4):[1]

Topical: "actions, attributes, or aspects" (*SHM* H 1075); concepts, objects (e.g., *–History, –Politics and government, –Social aspects*)

Figure 4.1. Topical subdivisions.
Lauren Enjeti.

Figure 4.2. Chronological subdivisions. *Lauren Enjeti.*

Chronological: time period, "usually associated with a historical treatment of a topic" (*SHM* H 1075) (e.g., *–20th century, –To 500, –1801-1917, –Tang-Five dynasties, 618-960*)

Figure 4.3. Geographic subdivisions. *Lauren Enjeti.*

Geographic: place, "where something is located, or where something is from, depending upon the topic" (*SHM* H 1075) (e.g., *–Florida, –Dallas (Tex.), –Mexico, –Michigan, Lake*)

Figure 4.4. Form subdivisions. *Lauren Enjeti.*

Form: what a resource is as opposed to what it is about (e.g., *–Pictorial works, –Dictionaries, –Juvenile fiction*)

In LCSH, subdivisions will always begin with a hyphen, sometimes long (–) and sometimes short (-), to distinguish them from main subject headings. Since LCSH was not designed to capture all angles of a topic in one main heading, subdivisions expand the meaning of the main heading, if needed. For example, if I want to make it clear that a resource is about fire departments in Florida, and not about fire departments everywhere in the world, I should include the geographic subdivision *–Florida* after the main heading *Fire departments* in the interest of specificity: *Fire departments–Florida.* You can include as many subdivisions as needed as long as you follow the instructions for constructing subject heading strings as presented in the *Subject Headings Manual.*

Sometimes you need only one subdivision to clearly express the topic, as in the case of the Florida fire departments above. At other times, multiple subdivisions may be needed. For example, if the resource I am cataloging is a directory of fire departments in Florida, and there is a valid subdivision for directories in LCSH (there is) that has a scope that includes this topic (it does—more on this in a moment), then it is fine to include it in my subject heading string as well: *Fire departments–Florida–Directories.*

I will talk more about the order of subdivisions shortly because there is a specific order you need to follow. But first I want to explain how to find subdivisions in LCSH because, just like the main subject headings, you cannot just make up any subdivision term you want!

LCSH includes quite a few subdivisions in the main LCSH list. If you perform a search in Classification Web for *Cats,* then click forward one page, you will see some main heading/subdivision entries (shown in figure 4.5). As mentioned previously, the entries in bold font are valid; those not in bold are invalid and provide the valid subject heading after *USE* (like USE *Feline diabetes* instead of *Cats–Diabetes*).

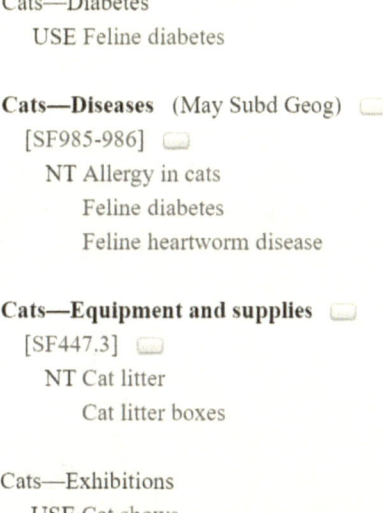

Cats—Diabetes
  USE Feline diabetes

Cats—Diseases (May Subd Geog)
  [SF985-986]
    NT Allergy in cats
    Feline diabetes
    Feline heartworm disease

Cats—Equipment and supplies
  [SF447.3]
    NT Cat litter
    Cat litter boxes

Cats—Exhibitions
  USE Cat shows

Figure 4.5. *Cats* **and subdivisions in Classification Web.** *Library of Congress.*

I will talk more about geographic headings and subdivisions in chapter 7, but it is important to mention the presence of *(May Subd Geog)* next to the *Cats–Diseases* entry in the example. *(May Subd Geog)* indicates that you can include a geographic subdivision immediately following this subject heading string. For example, if the item I am cataloging is about behavior therapy of cats in Florida, then I can safely place *–Florida*, a geographic subdivision, after *–Diseases*: *Cats–Diseases–Florida*.

On the other hand, note that *Cats–Equipment and supplies* does not have *(May Subd Geog)* after it. If an entry does not have *(May Subd Geog)* or has *(Not Subd Geog)*, that means that you cannot place a geographic subdivision after it. Chapter 7 will provide further guidance on the complex instructions associated with geographic subject headings and subdivisions.

Even though the main LCSH list contains quite a few subdivisions, it does not include them all. The practice of having a separate list of subdivisions was formalized in the 1970s, and **free-floating subdivisions** became commonly used with LCSH. According to the *Subject Headings Manual* H 1095—Free-Floating Subdivisions,

> The term **free-floating** refers to a form or topical subdivision that may be used under designated subjects without the usage being established editorially, and, as a consequence, without an authority record being created for each main heading/subdivision combination that might be needed.[2]

In other words, you can use free-floating subdivisions regardless of whether or not they appear in the main LCSH list—they "float" from subject heading string to subject heading string, depending on need and scope. However, as we will see, free-floating subdivisions cannot be used with just any subject heading. Often there are restrictions regarding the types of subject headings to which free-floating subdivisions can be assigned. I will come back to this idea once we explore how to find free-floating subdivisions.

For many years, the free-floating subdivisions were listed in a separate print volume. Currently, Library of Congress maintains the list entirely online. To access the free-floating subdivisions list in Classification Web, go to the main search page in LCSH and note the option for searching "Free-floating subdiv" (see figure 4.6). The free-floating subdivisions can be accessed free of charge in the LCSH document online: https://www.loc.gov/aba/publications/FreeLCSH/SUBDIVISIONS.pdf.

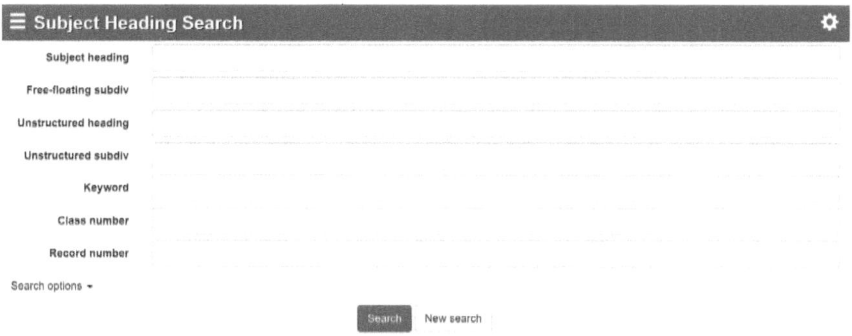

Subdivisions and Free-Floating Subdivisions 33

Figure 4.6. Subject heading search. *Library of Congress.*

Abbreviated lists are included in the *Subject Headings Manual*—H 1095 (Free-Floating Subdivisions: Form and Topical), H 1140 (Free-Floating Subdivisions: Names of Places), and H 1110 (Free-Floating Subdivisions: Names of Persons). Each of these lists is included at the end of this book, though without the additional scope notes and references to other *SHM* instructions.

As mentioned in the *SHM* definition of "free-floating" above, free-floating subdivisions are primarily topical and form. There are a few chronological subdivisions and no geographic subdivisions. Let's look at an example. Type in the popular free-floating subdivision *Fiction* in the free-floating subdivision search and click on "Search" (see figure 4.7). You should then see a search result screen that looks very similar to what

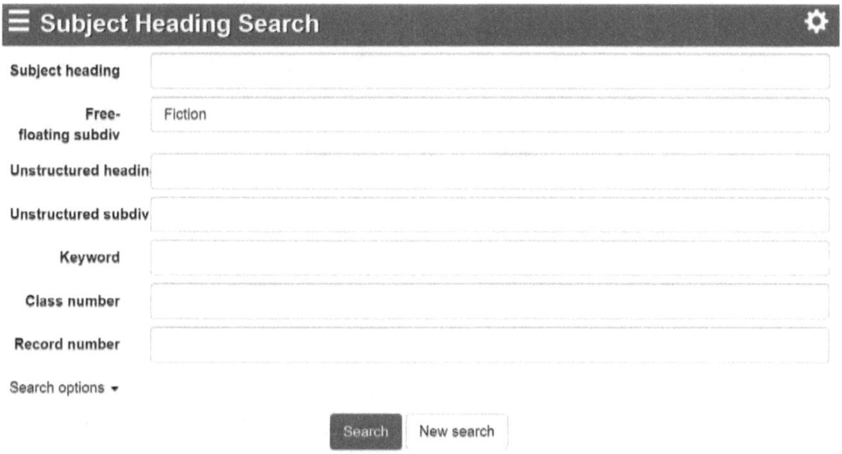

Figure 4.7. Free-floating subdivisions search for fiction. *Library of Congress.*

Sorted by Free-floating subdiv

—Fiction
Use as a form subdivision under names of countries, cities, etc., names of individual persons, families, and corporate bodies, and under classes of persons, ethnic groups, names of deities and mythological or legendary figures, individual and groups of fictitious and legendary characters, and topical headings for collections of stories or novels on those subjects. Also use under names of individual persons and historic events for individual works of biographical or historical fiction, and under animals for individual stories about animals.

UF —Legends and stories [Former subdivision]
   —Novels
   —Stories
NT —Juvenile fiction

Figure 4.8.   Fiction entry in the free-floating subdivisions list. *Library of Congress.*

we saw in the main LCSH list, but note the "Sorted by Free-floating subdiv" message at the top of the screen (see figure 4.8). Just like main headings in LCSH, valid subdivisions are in bold. The long hyphen preceding *Fiction* tells us that this is a subdivision and not a main heading. The free-floating subdivisions list contains the used for (UF), broader term (BT), narrower term (NT), and so on, like what we saw in the main LCSH list.

What is striking about the free-floating subdivision entries is the frequent inclusion of scope notes that not only clarify the type of subdivision (e.g., form or topical) but also provide usage restrictions. *–Fiction* actually has few restrictions since it can be used under names of countries, cities, etc., names of individual persons, families, and corporate bodies, and under classes of persons, ethnic groups, names of deities and mythological or legendary figures, individual and groups of fictitious and legendary characters, and topical headings for collections of stories or novels on those subjects. As long as the work you are cataloging is a collection of stories or a novel, you will most likely be able to place *–Fiction* in any subject heading string you want. Here are some examples:

cities	*Chicago (Ill.)–Fiction*
classes of persons	*Children–Fiction*
legendary characters	*Bunyan, Paul (Legendary character)–Fiction*
topical headings	*Dragons–Fiction*

However, not all free-floating subdivisions are that flexible, so you have to pay close attention to the scope notes. Figure 4.9 has a few more examples of free-floating subdivisions that have a more restricted scope. *–Breaking in* can be used only as a topical subdivision under individual

—**Brazing** (May Subd Geog)
   Use as a topical subdivision under individual metals and metal compounds.

—**Breaking in**
   Use as a topical subdivision under individual land vehicles and types of land vehicles.

—**Breath control**
   Use as a topical subdivision under individual musical instruments and familes of instruments.
   UF —Control, Breath

Figure 4.9. Free-floating subdivisions with restricted scope. *Library of Congress.*

land vehicles and types of land vehicles. Therefore, the following subject heading string is valid according to this scope: *Automobiles–Breaking in*. But this one is not: *Houses–Breaking in*.

Subdivisions are a critically important feature of LCSH that allow catalogers to narrow the focus of a topic. The rules associated with applying subdivisions can be quite complex, but they can be mastered by paying close attention to *Subject Headings Manual* instructions and scope notes associated with the subdivision. The next chapter will offer guidance on how to take what you have learned in the last few chapters and encode it in Machine-Readable Cataloging (MARC).

EXERCISES

Use Classification Web (or another source for finding LCSH if you cannot access Classification Web) to assign a Library of Congress subject heading and one or more subdivisions to the following works. Some, but not all, will require you to consult the Free-Floating Subdivisions list.

1. A work about collecting snow globes
2. A work about the grooming of sheep
3. A work about museums in France
4. A work about construction industry employees
5. A work of fiction about an only child that is meant for a juvenile audience
6. A work about medical care in the United States
7. A work on the fading of the color of corn

8. A work on dog parties of the twenty-first century
9. A book of poetry that is primarily about the size of raindrops
10. A dictionary of twentieth-century modernist art

NOTES

1. Library of Congress, "Subdivisions H 1075," *Subject Headings Manual*, last modified June 2013, https://www.loc.gov/aba/publications/FreeSHM/H1075.pdf.

2. Library of Congress, "Free-Floating Subdivisions H 1095," *Subject Headings Manual*, last modified November 2019, https://www.loc.gov/aba/publications/FreeSHM/H1095.pdf.

5

MARC Coding of LCSH

Let's say you go to your local library's website and search the catalog for the book *Rosa Parks: A Biography*. In addition to the information about the book's title, author, publisher, and number of pages, you should see fields that contain subject vocabularies like we have discussed in previous chapters:

Parks, Rosa, 1913-2005
African American women civil rights workers–Alabama–Montgomery
 –Biography
Civil rights movements–United States–History–20th century
Montgomery (Ala.)–Biography
Biography

However, behind the scenes of the library catalog, this same information looks a little different:

600 10 $a Parks, Rosa, $d 1913-2005
650 _0 $a African American women civil rights workers $z Alabama $z Montgomery $v Biography
650 _0 $a Civil rights movements $z United States $x History $y 20th century
651 _0 $a Montgomery (Ala.) $v Biography
655 _7 $a Biography. $2 lcgft

The additional numbers, dollar signs ($), and lowercase letters you see above are part of what is called **Machine-Readable Cataloging (MARC)**. MARC is the most commonly used encoding standard in library catalogs. Encoding standards are important because, in order for the catalog to work effectively, the information we create to describe resources needs to be in a syntax that computers understand and can act on. For example, by placing Rosa Parks's name in the MARC field 600, I am making it clear to the computer system that "Rosa Parks" is a person's name and not a geographic place (of course, *we* know this, but we cannot assume our computer systems do).

If your institution does not use the MARC standard or you are not interested in learning MARC, you can skip this chapter. However, I will use MARC coding in examples for the remainder of this book, so it might be worth it for you to read this chapter nonetheless! Classification Web does not contain MARC coding in the Library of Congress subject headings (LCSH) and Free-Floating Subdivisions lists, so you will need to determine what MARC coding is needed.

There are multiple MARC formats, but in this chapter I will discuss only "bibliographic" MARC—the MARC used to construct records in a library catalog. Therefore, whenever I use the term *MARC* in this chapter, assume I mean bibliographic MARC unless I state otherwise. I recommend consulting either the OCLC Bibliographic Formats and Standards website (https://www.oclc.org/bibformats/en.html) or the Library of Congress Bibliographic MARC website (http://www.loc.gov/marc/bibliographic/) to learn more about MARC and see further examples of its use.

MARC—THE BASICS

In MARC, there are multiple fields that can be used to convey subject information. Here are some common MARC subject field codes, always three digits in length:

600—personal name subject access point
610—corporate name subject access point
630—uniform title subject access point
650—topical subject access point

651—geographic access point
655—form/genre access point

MARC fields also contain two character positions immediately following the MARC field code, which are called indicators. If a MARC field contains values in the indicator spots (sometimes they do not), the value will be a single digit that has a different meaning depending on the field. In addition, each indicator is independent of the other—the meaning of one indicator does not influence the other. If you use LCSH to populate a MARC subject field, the second indicator will always be zero (0).

MARC fields also contain subfields that begin with a delimiter symbol (such as $, |, or ‡) and end with a lowercase letter (b, c, f, etc.) or a number (2, 4, etc.). Subfields will be particularly important in LCSH subject fields that contain subdivisions. Let's look at the most popular subfields within a MARC subject field.

$a contains the main subject heading and will have a different meaning depending on the field. For example, if a topical subject heading, such as *Dogs*, is in $a, use the MARC 650 field. When a person's name is in $a, such as *Washington, George, 1732-1799*, use the MARC 600 field.

$c designates titles and other words associated with a name. For example, the term of address *Jr.* is placed in $c ($a Connick, Harry, $c Jr., $d 1967-) and other words or phrases that provide more information about a name ($a Kermit, $c the Frog).

$d contains dates associated with what is in $a, such as birth and/or death dates or when a person was active (typically used when birth and death dates are unknown). These dates can be ascertained from an authority database. For example, in $a Shakespeare, William, $d 1564-1616, the years in $d state his birth year and death year.

$t provides the title of a work. For example, if a resource is about Shakespeare's play *Romeo and Juliet*, include both Shakespeare's name in $a and the title of the work in $t: $a Shakespeare, William, $d 1564-1616. $t Romeo and Juliet. This information can also be found in an authority database.

$v is used for **form subdivisions**, which are added to show that the work is in a particular physical or intellectual form, such as $v Maps or $v Fiction.

$x is used for **topical subdivisions** (concepts or objects), such as $x History or $x Collectibles.

$y is used for **chronological subdivisions**, which are added when a work is about a topic within a certain time period, such as $y 20th century.

$z is used for **geographic subdivisions**, which are added when a work emphasizes a particular geographic location, such as $z Texas.

Below, I will go through each of the common MARC subject fields as well as their respective indicators and subfields and provide examples. A word of caution: most of these MARC subject fields are populated using sources other than LCSH. For example, personal name, corporate name, conference title, and uniform titles (preferred titles of works) can be found using authority files, such as Library of Congress's authority file or OCLC's authority file. Form/genre headings, though still present to a certain extent in LCSH, are now mainly in the LC Genre/Form Terms for Library and Archival Materials (LCGFT), which is accessible via Classification Web, the LC Authorities website, or the LC Linked Data Service website. I will provide reminders of websites you should consult throughout my discussion of the different MARC subject fields below.

600—Personal Name Subject Access Point

Let's start with the 600 field. This field should be used if the resource is primarily about a person, like a biography or autobiography, a specific aspect of a person's life, or materials associated with a person. Additionally, the 600 field may be used when a resource features a real or fictional person as a main character or if a resource discusses the work(s) of a particular author. Chapter 8, "Personal Name Subject Headings and Biographies," will provide a more in-depth discussion of personal names as subjects.

It is good practice to use a personal name authorized access point in this field so that catalog users can find resources about a person consistently under one form of that person's name. For example, the authorized access point for the American author and poet Edgar Allan Poe is *Poe, Edgar Allan, 1809-1849*. His birth and death years are included to distinguish him from other people with the same name (and there are a few!). Many personal name authorized access points are documented in records within what are called authority files. Many libraries have their own authority

Figure 5.1. Edgar Allan Poe. *Lauren Enjeti.*

file, but Library of Congress and OCLC have their own authority files that are very popular. Consult chapter 8 of this book for more information about how to find and interpret name authority records.

The first indicator in the 600 field provides the type of personal name entry (0—forename; 1—surname; 3—family name). For example, personal names that have either a forename, initials, or a characterizing phrase in direct order should have "0" in the first indicator spot, e.g., 600 00 $a Winnie-the-Pooh $c (Fictitious character). Personal names in inverted order (surname, forename) should have "1" in the first indicator spot (e.g., 600 10 $a Austen, Jane, $d 1775-1817). Names of families, clans, dynasties, and the like should have "3" in the first indicator spot (e.g., 600 30 $a Kennedy family).

The second indicator specifies the controlled vocabulary used (0— Library of Congress subject headings).

The subfield codes will be the same as what is included in an authorized name access point ($a, $c, $d, etc.). Additional subfield codes may be added if a topical or form subdivision is included.

Title: *A Biography of George Washington, the First American President*
Subject: Washington, George, 1732-1799
In MARC:
600 10 $a Washington, George, $d 1732-1799

Title: *Edgar Allan Poe and the Jewel of Peru* (a mystery novel featuring Poe as a character)
Subject: Poe, Edgar Allan, 1809-1849–Fiction
In MARC:
600 10 $a Poe, Edgar Allan, $d 1809-1849 $v Fiction

Title: *Witness to the Journey: James Baldwin's Later Fiction*
Subject: Baldwin, James, 1924-1987–Criticism and interpretation
In MARC:
600 10 $a Baldwin, James, $d 1924-1987 $v Criticism and interpretation

Title: *Madonna: Blond Ambition* (a biography of American singer/actress Madonna)
Subject: Madonna, 1958-
In MARC:
600 00 $a Madonna, $d 1958-

610—Corporate Name Subject Access Point

The 610 field should be used if a corporate body is the subject of a resource. The first indicator provides the type of corporate body entry (0—inverted name; 1—jurisdiction name; 2—name in direct order), and the second indicator specifies the controlled vocabulary used (0—Library of Congress subject headings).

The subfield codes will be the same as what is included in an authorized corporate body access point ($a, $b, $d, etc.). Additional subfield codes may be included if a topical or form subdivision is needed.

Title: *An Inside Look at OCLC Online Computer Library Center*
Subject: OCLC
In MARC:
610 20 $a OCLC

Title: *The United States Supreme Court: Its History, Function, and Structure*
Subject: United States. Supreme Court
In MARC:
610 10 $a United States. $b Supreme Court

630—Uniform Title Subject Access Point

The 630 field should be used if a work is the subject of a resource but only when there is no name associated with the preferred title (see the 600 field if there is an author name as well). The first indicator tells the system how many nonfiling characters to skip (0—nonfiling characters; 1-9—number of nonfiling characters), and the second indicator specifies the controlled vocabulary used (0—Library of Congress subject headings). Nonfiling characters frequently refer to initial articles, such as *a*, *an*, or *the*, that should be ignored by the system for indexing purposes.

The subfield codes will be the same as what is included in an authorized title access point ($a, $b, $d, etc.). Additional subfield codes may be included if a topical or form subdivision is needed.

Title: *The Real Mother Goose*
Subject: Mother Goose
In MARC:
630 00 $a Mother Goose

Title: *Creating the World of Harry Potter*
Subject: Harry Potter and the sorcerer's stone (Motion picture)
In MARC:
630 00 $a Harry Potter and the sorcerer's stone (Motion picture)

650—Topical Subject Access Point

The 650 field should be used if a topic (object or concept) is the subject of a resource. The first indicator explains the level of the subject—if the subject term in the field is the primary subject of the work or the secondary subject. The first indicator in the 650 field is usually left blank if LCSH is used, but you may see a value in this indicator when other subject vocabularies are applied, such as the Medical Subject Headings. The second indicator specifies the controlled vocabulary used (0—Library of Congress subject headings).

Common subfield codes in the 650 field are $x (topical subdivision), $y (chronological subdivision), $z (geographic subdivision), and $v (form subdivision). You can have more than one type of subdivision in a subject heading string if it applies. For example, if a resource is both a pictorial work and a dictionary (both form subdivisions), you could assign this: $v Pictorial works $v Dictionaries.

In most cases, the preferred order of the subdivisions is as follows, if more than one subdivision is assigned, with $a first and $v (usually) last: 650 _0 $a [topic] $x [topic] $z [place] $y [chronological period] $v [form].

The order may shift around depending on what you are trying to convey or limitations presented by headings or subdivisions that cannot be subdivided geographically (more about this in chapter 7). In the *Subject Headings Manual* H 1075, the following example is provided:

650 _0 $a Hospitals $x Administration $x Data processing $x Evaluation
[Evaluation of the application of data processing to the administration of hospitals]
650 _0 $a Hospitals $x Administration $x Evaluation $x Data processing
[Application of data processing to the evaluation of the administration of hospitals]

Even though each of the above subject fields contains the same main heading and subdivisions, the slight modification of the order of the subdivisions changes the meaning of the field.

Title: *A Handbook on Managing Conflict*
Subject: Conflict management–Handbooks, manuals, etc.
In MARC:
650 _0 $a Conflict management $v Handbooks, manuals, etc.

Title: *I Grew Up to Be President*
Subject: Presidents–United States–Childhood and youth–Juvenile literature
In MARC (Normally the $z and $x subdivisions are flipped, but *$x Childhood* and *youth* cannot be subdivided geographically.):
650 _0 $a Presidents $z United States $x Childhood and youth $v Juvenile literature

Title: *The Modern Mind: An Intellectual History of the 20th Century*
Subject: Intellectual life–History–20th century
In MARC:
650 _0 $a Intellectual life $x History $y 20th century

651—Geographic Subject Access Point

The 651 field should be used if a geographic name is the main subject of a resource. I will provide a more in-depth discussion of what constitutes a geographic heading in chapter 7, so I recommend consulting that chapter if you are unsure whether or not a heading is geographic.

The first indicator in the 651 field should be left blank. The second indicator specifies the controlled vocabulary used (0—Library of Congress subject headings).

The same subfields that apply in the 650 field also apply here: $x (topical subdivision), $y (chronological subdivision), $z (geographic subdivision), and $v (form subdivision). According to the *Subject Headings Manual* H 1075, this is the typical order of a 651 field: 651 _0 $a [place] $x [topic] $y [chronological period] $v [form].

Title: *Fodor's Travel Guide to Chicago*
Subject: Chicago (Ill.)–Guidebooks
In MARC:
651 _0 $a Chicago (Ill.) $v Guidebooks

Title: *Who Owns Stonehenge?*
Subject: Stonehenge (England)–Claims
In MARC:
651 _0 $a Stonehenge (England) $x Claims

Title: *The Early Civilization of China*
Subject: China–Civilization–To 221 B.C.
In MARC:
651 _0 $a China $x Civilization $y To 221 B.C.

655—Form/Genre Access Point

The 655 field should be used if you want to highlight the form or genre of a resource. The Library of Congress broadly defines genres and forms as "categories of resources that share known conventions."[1] As I mentioned in chapter 2, "Basic Principles of Subject Analysis," form headings emphasize physical characteristics and what the resource *is*. Form examples include dictionaries, diaries, and maps. Genre headings emphasize themes in the intellectual content of a resource, such as technique or style. Genre examples include detective and mystery fiction, war films, and rock and roll music. I will discuss form/genre headings more within the context of fiction resources in chapter 9, "Fiction."

The first indicator in the 655 field should be left blank. The second indicator specifies the thesaurus used, but we have to be careful here. Use 0 in the second indicator if the genre/form heading is in LCSH, but there is not an abundance of genre/form headings in LCSH anymore. The Library of Congress has been slowly building its Library of Congress Genre/Form Terms (LCGFT) for Library and Archival Materials list to better represent genres/forms and keep them separated from LCSH, which focuses primarily on what a resource is *about* rather than what it *is* or into which genre it falls. If you use headings from LCGFT, the second indicator should be 7 (source is specified in subfield $2) and place $2 lcgft at the end of the heading after the period (e.g., 655 _7 $a Puzzles and games. $2 lcgft).

Genre/form headings should stand on their own and *not* be subdivided. For example, you *cannot* have 655 _7 $a Horror films $z Japan. $2 lcgft assigned to a Japanese horror movie. I recommend consulting the Library of Congress's free LCGFT documentation, specifically J 110—Assigning Genre/Form Terms.[2]

The LCGFT is accessible from the main menu of Classification Web (LC Genre/Form Terms) or through LC Authorities, the LC Linked Data Service, or the LCGFT website: https://www.loc.gov/aba/publications/FreeLCGFT/freelcgft.html.

> Title: *An Anthology of American Short Stories*
> Form/Genre: Short stories, American
> In MARC:
> 655 _0 $a Short stories, American

> Title: *Terribly Tricky Tongue Twisters*
> Form/Genre: Tongue twisters
> In MARC:
> 655 _7 $a Tongue twisters. $2 lcgft

MARC coding is still extremely popular in libraries even though it has been in existence since the 1960s. The granularity of MARC allows catalogers to encode Library of Congress subject heading strings, as well as other subject vocabularies, for machine readability. I have mentioned the *Subject Heading Manual* many times in this and previous chapters, so I would like to take a closer look at this important guide to LCSH in the next chapter.

EXERCISES

Use Classification Web (or another source for finding LCSH if you cannot access Classification Web) to assign a Library of Congress subject heading and one or more subdivisions to the following works. Some, but not all, will require you to consult the Free-Floating Subdivisions list. Only one subject heading string is needed per item. Encode the subject heading string in MARC.

1. A work on the history of butter carving
2. A work on the identification of the mountain lion
3. A work on pet food recipes

4. A work about the places frequented by American singer and actress Cher (her authorized access point is Cher, 1946-)
5. A work about pillage during the First World War
6. A manual on the prevention of attacks by bears
7. A work of fiction about the use of bees in war
8. A board book for young children
9. A work about games for children
10. A work about the social life and customs in New York City during the American colonial period. The authorized access point for New York City is New York (N.Y.).

NOTES

1. Library of Congress, "Introduction to Library of Congress Genre/Form Terms for Library and Archival Materials," last modified 2020, https://www.loc.gov/aba/publications/FreeLCGFT/2020%20LCGFT%20intro.pdf.

2. Library of Congress, "Assigning Genre/Form Terms—J110," last modified January 2016, https://www.loc.gov/aba/publications/FreeLCGFT/J110.pdf.

6

The *Subject Headings Manual* (*SHM*)

The *Subject Headings Manual* (*SHM*) is a handbook for Library of Congress subject headings (LCSH) published by the Library of Congress (LC) that was originally created for in-house LC cataloger use. When it was published for use outside of LC in 1984, it was titled *Subject Cataloging Manual: Subject Headings*. In 2008, the document was retitled as the *Subject Headings Manual*. You may still see references to the *SCM* rather than the *SHM*, but they refer to essentially the same document that has been updated continuously over the years of its existence.[1]

The *SHM* contains a lot of important information about LCSH, some of which I have already mentioned, such as the "20 percent rule" (*SHM* H 0180) and the order of subdivisions within a subject heading string (*SHM* H 1075). The *SHM* instructions are organized into individual documents that are listed in numerical order according to identifiers that begin with the letter "H" and then contain four numbers. The documents also have a title, such as "Order of Subject Headings," so they can be easily located by topic. The following image shows the top of the *SHM* web page (https://www.loc.gov/aba/publications/FreeSHM/freeshm.html), but you can also access the *SHM* through Cataloger's Desktop if you have a subscription to that resource (see figure 6.1).

In addition to providing general advice on constructing and assigning LCSH and subdivisions, the *SHM* provides instructions for assigning LCSH to specific types of resources or subject matter. For example, *SHM* H 1430 offers subject cataloging guidance on "comics and comic

List of the Subject Headings Manual PDF Files

H 0000 - H 0100 - H 0200 - H 0300 - H 0400 - H 0500 - H 0600 - H 0700 - H 0800 - H 0900 - H 1000 - H 1100 - H 1200 - H 1300 - H 1400 - H 1500 - H 1600 - H 1700 - H 1800 - H 1900 - H 2000 - H 2100 - H 2200 - H 2300 - H 2400; Glossary and Appendices -

H 0000

> **H 0040** Library of Congress Subject Authority Records *(PDF, 63 KB)* **REVISED January 2020**

> **H 0080** Order of Subject Headings *(PDF, 20 KB)*

⊕ Back to Top

H 0100

> **H 0150** Partial Title Added Entries *(PDF, 21 KB)*
> **H 0160** Uncontrolled Subject Terms in the 653 Field *(PDF, 42 KB)*
> **H 0165** Subject Heading Changes in Bibliographic Records *(PDF, 39 KB)* **REVISED January 2020**
> **H 0170** CONSER & BIBCO Standard Records *(PDF, 131 KB)*
> **H 0175** Editions *(PDF, 21 KB)*
> **H 0178** Serials *(PDF, 20 KB)*
> **H 0180** Assigning and Constructing Subject Headings *(PDF, 53 KB)* **REVISED**

Figure 6.1. *Subject Headings Manual. Library of Congress.*

characters," and *SHM* H 1690 covers "juvenile materials." Instead of delving into every *SHM* instruction, I will discuss the more general rules and encourage you to explore the *SHM* on your own so you have a better understanding of its coverage. The exercises at the end of this chapter will help you get started exploring the nooks and crannies of *SHM*. I recommend that you follow along in the *SHM* as I go through specific *SHM* instruction sheets below.

The *SHM* contains guidance not only on assigning existing LCSH and subdivisions but also on how to create new headings and subdivisions. *SHM* H 0200 (Preparation of Subject Heading Proposals) provides a step-by-step guide to preparing a subject heading proposal if you want LC to consider *adding* a subject heading or subdivision. The *SHM* has separate instructions (H 0193–H 1096) for proposals to *modify* existing subject headings or subdivisions. *SHM* H 0202 through H 0205 also provide direction in this area, including authority research for subject heading proposals, citation of sources, and how LC evaluates subject proposals when they are received. If you are interested in adding or modifying LC subject headings and subdivisions but are new to the process and uncertain about how to get started, I recommend visiting the Cataloging Lab (http://cataloginglab.org/), a crowdsourced project that has put forward several successful proposals.

SHM H 0285 (Singular vs. Plural Forms in Subject Headings) provides helpful information for when you are searching or creating headings for LCSH. The general rule states that one should "use the plural form when establishing topical headings that designate entities capable of being enumerated. Use the singular form when establishing topical headings that designate abstract concepts."[2] In other words, concepts and objects that can be counted should be plural subject headings (*Dogs*, *Presidents*), but abstract concepts that cannot be counted should be singular (*Love*, *Classification*).

SHM H 0180 (Assigning and Constructing Subject Headings) has a lot of fantastic information about LCSH, including discussions of specificity and depth of indexing that I noted in chapter 1, "Library of Congress Subject Headings in a Nutshell." H 0180 also contains guidance on what heading(s) to assign resources that are about multiple topics, which can be a bit confusing, so I would like to spend some time discussing these instructions.

SHM H 0180 section 7 (Two or Three Related Headings) states that "if a heading exists, or can be established, that represents the two or three topics discussed in a work, and that includes no other topics within its scope, assign the one heading instead of two or three narrower headings."[3] Though not clearly articulated, this instruction should be applied only when a resource is about two or three related topics within a broader topic that contains only two or three subtopics. For example, if a book is about dog collars and dog leashes, this rule recommends that you assign *Dogs—Equipment and supplies* rather than the more specific *Dog collars* and *Dog leashes* because these are the only two subtopics (narrower terms) under the broader subject heading string *Dogs—Equipment and supplies*. Figure 6.2 shows section 7 in *SHM* H 0180.

On the other hand, *SHM* H 0180 section 8 (The "Rule of Three") states that "if a general topic includes in its scope more than three subtopics,

7. Two or three related headings. If a heading exists, or can be established, that represents the two or three topics discussed in a work, and that includes no other topics within its scope, assign the one heading instead of two or three narrower headings. *Examples:*

Title: By land, sea, and air : the story of transportation.
650 #0 $a Transportation $x History.

Title: In praise of single parents : mothers and fathers embracing the challenge.
650 #0 $a Single parents $z United States.

[*not* 650 #0 $a Single mothers $z United States.
650 #0 $a Single fathers $z United States.]

Figure 6.2. *SHM* H 0180, section 7 (Two or Three Related Headings). *Library of Congress.*

but the work being cataloged discusses only two or three of these subtopics, assign the appropriate two or three headings rather than the broader heading."[4] Apply this rule if a broader topic contains more than three subtopics, but only two or three of the subtopics are discussed in the resource. For example, if I am cataloging a book about ice cream sandwiches, snow cones, and ice cream, I should *not* assign the LCSH *Frozen desserts* but instead assign separate headings for *Ice cream, ices, etc.*; *Ice cream sandwiches*; and *Snow cones*, all narrower terms under the broader *Frozen desserts*. This is because *Frozen desserts* has more than three subtopics in LCSH. (See figure 6.3.)

Figure 6.3. My favorite frozen desserts. *Lauren Enjeti.*

SHM H 0180 section 9 (The "Rule of Four") provides an exception to the "rule of three" if a resource is about four specific topics within a very broad subject area. The example provided in the *SHM* is a resource that is about four American literary authors. Instead of assigning the subject heading string *American literature–History and criticism*, the *SHM* recommends assigning the authorized headings for the four authors instead. However, four is LC's limit for assigning specific headings. LC instructs its catalogers: "Do not exceed four subtopics under any circumstances."[5]

I will now discuss one final *SHM* rule about assigning LCSH to resources that are about multiple topics: *SHM* H 0180 section 10 (Multi-element Topics). This section states that "if a work discusses a complex or compound topic for which a single heading neither exists nor can be practically constructed or established, assign multiple headings to bring out the separate aspects of the topic."[6] As we discussed in chapter 2, "Basic Principles of Subject Analysis," it is inevitable that resources will be about topics that cannot be captured in one subject heading, so multiple headings must be assigned. LC uses the cheery example of cancer morbidity and mortality among Danish brewery workers to illustrate this point. There is not a single subject heading or subject heading string that we can use to capture the main topics of this work, so separate subject fields are necessary:

Cancer–Denmark
Cancer–Mortality–Denmark
Brewery workers–Diseases–Denmark
Brewery workers–Mortality–Denmark

In MARC:

650 _0 $a Cancer $z Denmark
650 _0 $a Cancer $x Mortality $z Denmark
650 _0 $a Brewery workers $x Diseases $z Denmark
650 _0 $a Brewery workers $x Mortality $z Denmark

Moving on to other topics, *SHM* H 1146 (Subdivisions Controlled by Pattern Headings) is particularly helpful when determining appropriate subdivisions. There are so many subdivisions available that it can be overwhelming trying to find one that fits your particular resource. **Pattern headings** are designated headings within specific topic areas that are followed by free-floating subdivisions appropriate to that topic area within LCSH. As long as the topic you are trying to find is within the chosen categories of pattern headings, you will see the range of possible free-floating subdivisions for that topic.

Let's say you are cataloging a book on the use of railroad transportation during World War I. You are pretty confident that the main LCSH should be *World War, 1914-1918* (the valid LCSH for World War I), but you are not certain which subdivision is appropriate for the concept of "railroad transportation." According to *SHM* H 1146, the "Wars" topic area has two pattern headings: *World War, 1939-1945* and *United States–History–Civil War, 1861-1865*—the subject heading strings for World War II and the American Civil War, respectively. If you go to either of those entries in LCSH, you will see they each have *–Railroads* and a USE *–Transportation* (*World War, 1939-1945–Transportation* and *United States–History–Civil War, 1861-1865–Transportation*). Therefore, using the logic of pattern headings, if *–Transportation* is valid as a subdivision for railroad transportation after these two wars, then it is fine to use *–Transportation* after *World War, 1914-1918*. (See figure 6.4.)

You may also notice that each of the pattern headings spans many pages because of the number of subdivisions that are included. *SHM* H 1146 gives further details about pattern headings, and *SHM* H 1147–H 1200 contains information about specific pattern headings that have been established.

Finally, the *SHM* glossary and appendices are useful if you are uncertain about how LC defines terms used in the *SHM*, such as *main entry* or *reference source* (glossary), capitalization of headings and subdivisions (Appendix B: Capitalization), and punctuation and spacing (Appendix D: Punctuation).

World War, 1939-1945—Railroads
    USE World War, 1939-1945—Transportation

World War, 1939-1945—Reconnaissance operations
    NT World War, 1939-1945—Bomb reconnaissance

World War, 1939-1945—Reconnaissance operations, American, [German, etc.]

World War, 1939-1945—Reconstruction
    USE Reconstruction (1939-1951)

Figure 6.4. World War, 1939–1945 entries. *Library of Congress.*

The Subject Headings Manual *(SHM)*

The *SHM* provides a plethora of guidance and examples that should make assigning and creating LCSH and subdivisions much easier and more understandable, particularly because LCSH offers little direction in the list itself. The exercises for this chapter will provide additional guidance on *SHM* content. The next chapter will delve more deeply into a topic we have only been dipping our toe into so far: geographic headings and subdivisions.

EXERCISES

Consult the *Subject Headings Manual* to answer the following questions.

1. What is the *SHM* instruction number associated with guidance on the following topics or type of materials?
   a. Songs and music
   b. Artistic photography
   c. Government publications
   d. Emigration and immigration
   e. Translations
2. Use H 0180 (Assigning and Constructing Subject Headings) to answer the following questions:
   a. According to section 12 (Concepts in Titles), if the title of the work is general, but the actual content of the work is specific, what heading(s) should you assign to the work?
   b. According to section 4 (Specificity), when is it appropriate to assign a broader or more general heading to a work about a more specific topic?
   c. If I am cataloging a work titled *The Best Tea Making Paraphernalia: Balls, Bowls, and Cozies*, do I assign to this work the LCSH *Tea making paraphernalia*?
   d. You are cataloging a work titled *Grandfathers and Grandmothers: Guidance on Your New Family Role*. Is it appropriate to assign the headings *Grandmothers–Family relationships* and *Grandfathers–Family relationships* to this work?

3. What is/are the pattern heading(s) for the following topics:
   a. Animals
   b. Plants and crops
   c. Legal topics
   d. Religions
4. Identify the *SHM* rule that applies to the creation of subject headings related to specific events, and answer the following questions, providing the section numbers that led to your answer:
   a. Should *State Fair of Texas* be established as a name heading or a subject heading?
   b. Should *Riots* be established as a name heading or a subject heading?
   c. If you are cataloging a book about the Zoot Suit Riots that occurred in Los Angeles, California, in 1943, how would you formulate that heading?
5. Identify the *SHM* rule that applies to pictorial works, and answer the following questions, providing the section numbers that led to your answer:
   a. I am cataloging a book about rainbows that consists entirely of pictures of rainbows. Is this subject heading string sufficient? *Rainbows–Pictorial works*.
   b. I am cataloging a book about rainbows that contains a substantial amount of text, but it also contains a lot of pictures (at least 50 percent of the book) and the illustrator is given special credit. Is this subject heading string sufficient? *Rainbows–Pictorial works*.
6. I am cataloging a work on the professional ethics of librarians in East Germany, when it was the German Democratic Republic. Find the *SHM* rule and section that will help me determine what to assign for the geographic aspect of this work and then pick which subject heading string below is correct according to the *SHM* instructions:

Librarians–Professional ethics–Germany
Librarians–Professional ethics–Germany (East)
Librarians–Professional ethics–Germany (Democratic Republic, 1949-)

NOTES

1. Library of Congress, "About the Subject Headings Manual PDF Files," last modified October 2014, https://www.loc.gov/aba/publications/FreeSHM/freeshmabout.html.

2. Library of Congress, "Singular vs. Plural Forms in Subject Headings–H 0285," *Subject Headings Manual*, last modified June 2013, https://www.loc.gov/aba/publications/FreeSHM/H0285.pdf.

3. Library of Congress, "Assigning and Constructing Subject Headings–H 0180," *Subject Headings Manual*, last modified February 2016, https://www.loc.gov/aba/publications/FreeSHM/H0180.pdf.

4. Library of Congress, "Assigning and Constructing Subject Headings–H 0180."

5. Library of Congress, "Assigning and Constructing Subject Headings–H 0180."

6. Library of Congress, "Assigning and Constructing Subject Headings–H 0180."

7

Geographic Subject Headings and Subdivisions

Geographic subject headings and subdivisions are used when a geographic location is featured prominently. The *Subject Headings Manual* H 0690 (Formulating Geographic Headings) states that geographic name headings fall into two categories: (1) names of political jurisdictions and (2) nonjurisdictional geographic names.

Typically, political jurisdictions are places that are defined governmentally, such as cities, provinces, states, counties, regions, and countries. These include not only the actual geographic locations, e.g., *Dallas (Tex.)*, a city, but also the government of that location, e.g., *Dallas (Tex.). City Council*. However, the latter are considered corporate name headings, so for the purposes of this book, we will focus our attention on the former: geographic places.

In addition to the names of political jurisdictions, geographic headings can also be nonjurisdictional. In other words, they are geographic features or locations that do not have a political identity. *SHM* H 0690 contains a representative list of these types of places:[1]

- archaeological sites, historic sites, and so on
- areas and regions (when not free-floating)
- canals
- dams
- extinct cities (pre-1500)
- farms, ranches, gardens

- forests, grasslands, and so on
- geographic features (e.g., caves, deserts, nonjurisdictional islands, lakes, mountains, ocean currents, plains, rivers, seas, steppes, undersea features)
- geologic basins, geologic formations, and so on
- mines
- parks, reserves, refuges, recreation areas, and so on
- reservoirs
- roads, streets, trails
- valleys

Therefore, don't assume that a geographic heading can be only the name of a city, state, province, or country.

Geographic headings that fall within the first category (names of political jurisdictions) are constructed using descriptive cataloging standards. As of this writing, the main standard providing guidance in this area is *Resource Description and Access (RDA)*. Geographic headings that fall within the second category (nonjurisdictional geographic names) are constructed using the *Subject Headings Manual* (*SHM*) H 0690 (Formulating Geographic Headings).

Since this book is geared primarily toward those who are *assigning* rather than *creating* subject headings, I will not delve too deeply into the many instructions in RDA and the *SHM* for establishing geographic name headings. Instead, I will touch on the instructions in the aforementioned resources that are most important to understand so that the headings can be easily found. In addition, I will need to provide more information about finding and understanding authority records so you can determine the authorized forms of geographic headings and how to construct geographic subdivisions. Let's start with authority records.

Library of Congress subject headings (LCSH) contains a few, but not all, geographic headings. You will need to consult an authority file, such as Library of Congress's Authorities website or OCLC's authority file, to find valid geographic headings and subdivisions. Authority files contain **authority records** that document information about a specific agent (e.g., person, corporate body, family), title (e.g., work, series), or subject. Authority records do not document *all* information about a specific person, subject, or title. Instead, authority records contain the authorized access point, variant forms, and often other information that should be used for the purpose of identification. According to RDA (the descriptive cataloging standard mentioned earlier), an **authorized access point** is "a standardized access point representing an entity."[2] A **variant access point** is "an alternative to an authorized access point representing an entity."[3] For example, the authorized access point for the pop singer Lady Gaga is *Lady Gaga*, and a variant access point is her real name inverted: *Germanotta, Stefani*.

Identifying authorized and variant access points is important because it is easier to find resources by subject, author, or title if we search under one form of the term or name. In other words, you do not have to guess if Lady Gaga's latest album is under *Lady Gaga* or *Germanotta, Stefani*.

Authority records document this standardization and the sources used to determine which names are included. Geographic names are no exception. Figure 7.1 shows the authority record for the US city Dallas in the state of Texas, from the Library of Congress Authorities website. *Geographic heading* contains the authorized access point for Dallas, there is a variant form next to *Variant(s)*, and note the label *Geographic subdivision usage*, which tells us how to structure this place as subdivisions (minus the long hyphens and MARC coding). In the MARC format for authority data (which is different from the MARC discussed in chapter 5, "MARC Coding of LCSH"), the above authority record is shown in figure 7.2.

I recommend consulting the Library of Congress's MARC21 Format for Authority Data website to find out more about each field (https://www.loc.gov/marc/authority/). To avoid getting too far off track, let's focus on a few of the most important fields. The 151 field of the authority

LC control no.: n 79023321
LCCN Permalink: https://lccn.loc.gov/n79023321
Descriptive conventions: rda
Geographic heading: Dallas (Tex.)
Geographic subdivision usage: Texas Dallas
Variant(s): City of Dallas (Tex.)
Associated country: United States
Located: Texas
Type of jurisdiction: Cities and towns
County seats
Found in: GeoNames, algorithmically matched, 2009 (ppl; 32°46′59″N 096°48′24″W)
Wikipedia, July 10, 2019 (Dallas; City of Dallas; city in the U.S. state of Texas and the seat of Dallas County, with portions extending into Collin, Denton, Kaufman and Rockwall counties; 32°46′45″N 96°48′32″W)
Geographic area code: n-us-tx

Figure 7.1. Dallas (Tex.) authority record. *Library of Congress.*

```
LC control no.: n 79023321
LCCN Permalink: https://lccn.loc.gov/n79023321
    HEADING: Dallas (Tex.)
        000 01126cz a2200277n 450
        001 1886404
        005 20190712073143.0
        008 790418n| azannaabn |a ana
        010 __ |a n 79023321
        034 __ |d W0964824 |e W0964824 |f N0324659 |g N0324659 |2 geonames
        034 __ |d W0964832 |e W0964832 |f N0324645 |g N0324645 |2 wikiped
        034 __ |d W0970001 |e W0962749 |f N0330126 |g N0323647 |2 bound
        034 __ |d -097.000482 |e -096.463632 |f 033.023937 |g 032.613216 |2 bound
        035 __ |a (OCoLC)oca00257086
        040 __ |a DLC |b eng |e rda |c DLC |d WaU |d OCoLC |d DLC |d WaU
        043 __ |a n-us-tx
        151 __ |a Dallas (Tex.)
        368 __ |b Cities and towns |2 lcsh
        368 __ |b County seats |2 aat
        370 __ |c United States |e Texas |2 naf
        451 __ |a City of Dallas (Tex.)
        670 __ |a GeoNames, algorithmically matched, 2009 |b (ppl; 32°46'59"N 096°48'24"W)
        670 __ |a Wikipedia, July 10, 2019 |b (Dallas; City of Dallas; city in the U.S. state of Texas and the seat of
            Dallas County, with portions extending into Collin, Denton, Kaufman and Rockwall counties;
            32°46'45"N 96°48'32"W)
        781 _0 |z Texas |z Dallas
        952 __ |a RETRO
        953 __ |a xx00 |b rf08
```

Figure 7.2.   Dallas (Tex.) authority record in MARC. *Library of Congress.*

record contains the authorized access point, the 451 field(s) contain variant forms, and the 781 field tells us how to structure and code the place as subdivisions.

For example, let's say I am cataloging a book about the history of Dallas, Texas. Since the main focus of the work is a geographic place, I need to assign the placename that is located in the 151 field of the authority record, *Dallas (Tex.)*, and then subdivide it using the free-floating subdivision *–History*:

Dallas (Tex.)–History

Peeking back at chapter 5 of this book to remember the MARC coding, I see that I should code this subject heading string like this in the bibliographic record, using the MARC field code 651 for geographic subject headings: 651 _0 $a Dallas (Tex.) $x History.

There are many other free-floating subdivisions I can assign to a geographic main heading. I recommend consulting the *SHM* H 1140 (Free-Floating Subdivisions: Names of Places) to see the breadth of topics.

These subdivisions are also conveniently listed at the end of this book, though without the additional scope notes and references to other *SHM* instructions. What if another book crosses my desk, this time a book about gardens in Dallas, Texas? See figure 7.3.

In this book, the focus is gardens, but I want to make it clear that it is not about gardens anywhere and everywhere but in Dallas, Texas, specifically. After checking Classification Web to confirm that *Gardens* is a valid LCSH (it is), I need to refer to the 781 field of the *Dallas (Tex.)* authority record to see how it should be constructed as subdivisions. If I am not using MARC, I can ignore the $z subfield codes and place the geographic subdivisions after *Gardens* with long hyphens separating each term: *Gardens–Texas–Dallas*.

Figure 7.3. The Big "G"s of Big "D": Lovely Gardens of Dallas. Lauren Enjeti.

If I use MARC, then retain the MARC subfield codes and place *$z Texas $z Dallas* after *Gardens* in the subject heading string: 650 _0 $a Gardens $z Texas $z Dallas.

I would like to now circle back to the *Subject Headings Manual*, particularly *SHM* H 0830 (Geographic Subdivision), to discuss geographic subdivisions in more depth. As you can see from the Dallas, Texas, examples above, geographic subdivisions in LCSH are often *indirect*, meaning that a larger geographic entity is transcribed first in a subject heading string (like $z Texas, a US state) and a smaller geographic entity is transcribed last (like $z Dallas, a city). Other geographic subdivisions are *direct*, meaning you do not have to include larger and smaller geographic entities but assign only the larger geographic entity, like 650_ 0 $a Gardens $z United States or 650 _0 $a Gardens $z Washington (D.C.). The general provision in *SHM* H 0830 is shown in figure 7.4.

In other words, if a resource is about a topic that emphasizes a geographic area, the first geographic subdivision should be the country name,

1. General provision. When a heading is coded **(May Subd Geog)**, subdivide it directly by names of continents, regions larger than countries, countries, the provinces of Canada, the constituent countries of Great Britain, or the states of the United States. As a general rule, subdivide to subordinate localities located wholly within a country by interposing the name of the relevant country between the heading and the name of the subordinate locality. Subordinate localities include:

- subordinate political jurisdictions, such as provinces, districts, counties, cities, etc.
- historic kingdoms, principalities, etc.
- geographic features and regions, such as mountain ranges, bodies of water, lake regions, watersheds, metropolitan areas, etc.
- islands situated within the territorial limits of the country in question

Figure 7.4. General provision in *SHM* H 0830. *Library of Congress*.

then the next geographic subdivision should be the smallest geographic place named (such as a city, county, district, etc.). In addition, never include more than two geographic subdivisions per subject heading string. In a nutshell:

- Use the country name in the first geographic subdivision, then the smaller geographic area in the second (except for the United States and Canada—more on these two in a moment).
- Do not assign more than two geographic subdivisions per subject heading string.

For example, a book on gardens in the city of Ciudad Juarez, which is in the state of Chihuahua in Mexico (a country), should be assigned the following subject heading string:

Gardens–Mexico–Ciudad Juarez
650 _0 $a Gardens $z Mexico $z Ciudad Juarez

On the other hand, if a resource is about a topic that emphasizes a geographic area within the United States or Canada, the first geographic subdivision should be the US state or Canadian province (if the geographic emphasis is on the United States or Canada generally, then of course put *–United States* or *–Canada*). This is why in the *Dallas (Tex.)* authority record mentioned previously said to put *–Texas–Dallas* rather than *–United States–Dallas* or *–United States–Texas–Dallas*.

Below are further examples—once again, consult the 781 field of the authority record for each place to confirm how to transcribe the geographic subdivisions:

Gardens–British Columbia–Vancouver
650 _0 $a Gardens $z British Columbia $z Vancouver

Gardens–New York (State)–New York
650 _0 $a Gardens $z New York (State) $z New York

Geographic subdivisions should follow topical subject headings and subdivisions in a subject heading string, as mentioned earlier: 650 _ 0 $a [topic] $x [topic] $z [place] $y [chronological period] $v [form].

You may also recall that I mentioned that the presence of *(May Subd Geog)* indicates that you can include a geographic subdivision immediately following a heading or subdivision. If an entry does not have *(May Subd Geog)* or has *(Not Subd Geog)*, that means that you *cannot* place a geographic subdivision after it. For example, I noted that *Cats–Equipment and supplies* does *not* have *(May Subd Geog)* after it when I showed you the *Cats* example in chapter 4, "Subdivisions and Free-Floating Subdivisions." Figure 7.5 shows it again.

The *SHM* H 1075 (Subdivisions) explains that you can change the order of subdivisions if you are not able to subdivide a topical heading or subdivision but still need to include the geographic aspect.

Let's say you need to create a subject heading string for a resource about cat supplies in the United States. *Cats–Equipment and supplies* does not have *(May Subd Geog)* next to it, so you cannot place *–United States*

Cats—Diabetes
   USE Feline diabetes

Cats—Diseases (May Subd Geog)
   [SF985-986]
     NT Allergy in cats
     Feline diabetes
     Feline heartworm disease

Cats—Equipment and supplies
   [SF447.3]
     NT Cat litter
     Cat litter boxes

Cats—Exhibitions
   USE Cat shows

Figure 7.5. Cats and subdivisions in Classification Web. *Library of Congress.*

Figure 7.6. Cat and its equipment and supplies. *Lauren Enjeti.*

immediately after *–Equipment and supplies*: *Cats–Equipment and supplies–United States* (no!). But you can place *–United States* after *Cats* because it can be subdivided geographically: *Cats–United States–Equipment and supplies* (yes!).

As long as the heading or subdivision that immediately precedes the geographic subdivision can be subdivided geographically, then your subject heading string will be valid. (See figure 7.6.)

Geographic subject headings and subdivisions are not always needed in subject fields, but they are important to include when a resource is significantly about a geographic location (e.g., a history of a country, a travel guidebook for a city) or when a geographic location is an important aspect of the resource, even if it is not the primary focus (e.g., gardens in Dallas, Texas). When using geographic headings and subdivisions, you should consult authority records to confirm the authorized access point and valid order of subdivisions. Consulting authority records is also a good idea when assigning personal name subject headings, which is the subject of our next chapter. Join me after you complete the chapter 7 exercises!

EXERCISES

Use Classification Web (or another source for finding LCSH if you cannot access Classification Web) to assign a LC subject heading and one or more subdivisions to the following works. Some, but not all, will require you to consult the Free-Floating Subdivisions list. Consult the Library of Congress Authorities website (http://authorities.loc.gov/) or another authority file to determine the authorized geographic heading or subdivisions. Only one subject heading string is needed per item. If you prefer, encode the subject heading string in MARC. Some questions will require you to consult the *Subject Headings Manual*.

1. A work about krump dancing in Toronto, Canada
2. A directory of dog parks in Seattle, Washington
3. A periodical about employees in the sugar industry in Tokyo, Japan
4. A work on the study and teaching of hippotherapy in the United States
5. A travel guidebook for Rome, Italy
6. A work on the effect of inflation on life insurance in Santa Fe, New Mexico
7. A work about the evaluation of elementary schools in Minneapolis, Minnesota
8. A work on politics in Lisbon, Portugal, during the seventeenth century
9. A fiction work aimed at juveniles about collecting Hot Wheels toy cars in Canada
10. A work that consists of statistics on the reliability of rainfall in Rio de Janeiro, Brazil
11. A work on playing the children's game Chutes and Ladders in India
12. A work on artificial satellites orbiting the planet Mars

NOTES

1. Library of Congress, "Formulating Geographic Headings—H 0690," *Subject Headings Manual*, last modified June 2014, https://www.loc.gov/aba/publications/FreeSHM/H0690.pdf.

2. RDA Steering Committee, "Authorized Access Point," *RDA Toolkit*, last modified April 2017, http://access.rdatoolkit.org/.

3. RDA Steering Committee, "Variant Access Point," *RDA Toolkit*, last modified April 2017, http://access.rdatoolkit.org/.

8

Personal Name Subject Headings and Biographies

Personal name subject headings are commonly assigned to resources that are about a person, feature a person prominently (like in a novel or movie), or are about a person's work. Resources may also focus on a particular aspect of a person's life and work or materials associated with the person. This chapter will focus primarily on assigning personal name subject headings for biographical or autobiographical works but will also cover other instances when these subject headings are useful.

The chapter of this book on MARC (chapter 5) provides several examples of resources that contain personal name subject headings. Like we did for geographic subject headings and subdivisions, we should consult name authority records to determine the authorized access point for a person, which are constructed currently

```
         LC control no.: n 79029745
         LCCN Permalink: https://lccn.loc.gov/n79029745
  Descriptive conventions: rda
         LC classification: PS2600 PS2648
  Personal name heading: Poe, Edgar Allan, 1809-1849
              Variant(s): Po, Edgar, 1809-1849
                          Boy, Etkar, 1809-1849
                          Poe, E. A. (Edgar Allan), 1809-1849
                          Poë, Edgard, 1809-1849
                          Pui, ʻAggā ʻAyʻlanʻ, 1809-1849
                          Pō, Edgār Ālen, 1809-1849
                          Po, Edhar, 1809-1849
       Associated country: United States
              Birth date: 1809-01-19
              Death date: 1849-10-07
            Place of birth: Boston (Mass.)
           Place of death: Baltimore (Md.)
           Other attribute: Americans
 Profession or occupation: Authors Soldiers Poets
            Special note: Machine-derived non-Latin script reference project.
                          Non-Latin script references not evaluated.
                Found in: His Poems and tales ... 1902.
                          His Anastatic printing, 1972: t.p. (E.A. Poe)
                          Milhaud, D. Les cloches, c1960: t.p. (Edgard Poë)
                          Lyhuiʻ vhakʻ sai phui, 195-?: t.p. (ʻAggā ʻAyʻlanʻ Pui)
                          Suvarṇa kīta, 1947: t.p. (Edgār Āllen Pō)
                          Kruk, 2000: t.p. (Edhar Po)
                          The raven, 1883: t.p. (Edgar Allen Poe )
```

Figure 8.1. Edgar Allan Poe authority record. Library of Congress.

100 1_ |a Poe, Edgar Allan, |d 1809-1849
368 __ |c Americans |2 lcdgt
370 __ |a Boston (Mass.) |b Baltimore (Md.) |c United States |2 naf
374 __ |a Authors |a Soldiers |a Poets |2 lcsh
375 __ |a Males |2 lcdgt
377 __ |a eng
400 1_ |a Po, Edgar, |d 1809-1849
400 1_ |a Boy, Ētkar, |d 1809-1849
400 1_ |a Poe, E. A. |q (Edgar Allan), |d 1809-1849
670 __ |a His Poems and tales ... 1902.
670 __ |a His Anastatic printing, 1972: |b t.p. (E.A. Poe)
670 __ |a Milhaud, D. Les cloches, c1960: |b t.p. (Edgard Poë)
670 __ |a Lyhui' vhak' sai phui, 195-?: |b t.p. ('Aggā 'Ay'laṅ' Pui)
670 __ |a Suvarṇa kīṭa, 1947: |b t.p. (Eḍgār Āllen Pō)
670 __ |a Kruk, 2000: |b t.p. (Edhar Po)
670 __ |a The raven, 1883: |b t.p. (Edgar Allen Poe)

Figure 8.2. Edgar Allan Poe authority record in MARC. *Library of Congress.*

using *Resource Description and Access (RDA)* guidelines. You can use Library of Congress's authority file (http://authorities.loc.gov/) or any other authority file to find authority records. Since I used Edgar Allan Poe as an example in chapter 5, let's return to our macabre American author and poet. Figure 8.1 is an abbreviated version of his authority record on the Library of Congress's Authorities website without the MARC coding. Note his authorized access point next to the label "Personal name heading" and the many variant forms of his name. Figure 8.2 is the MARC coded version of Poe's authority record that is (once again) abbreviated for the sake of space.

I recommend consulting the Library of Congress's MARC21 Format for Authority Data website to find out more about each field (https://www.loc.gov/marc/authority/). Instead of going over every field, let's focus on the few that are most important for our purposes in this chapter. The 100 field of the authority record contains the personal name authorized access point, 400 fields contain variant forms of the name, and the 3xx fields (368, 370, etc.) provide additional information that is helpful for identification (we want to make sure to choose the correct Poe!). In this example, the authorized access point is *Poe, Edgar Allan, 1809-1849* or (in MARC) 100 1_ $a Poe, Edgar Allan, $d 1809-1849—the Edgar Allan Poe who wrote *The Raven*.

Personal name subject headings are important to include in records for biographies, autobiographies, and memoirs as well as other types of works associated with a person. This chapter will focus primarily on the former types of resources, but before we dive into that discussion, let's take some time to explore the latter: the "other" types of works that feature a person but may not be a full biography, autobiography, or memoir. For instance, in chapter 5, "MARC Coding of LCSH," I provided the following example:

Title: *Witness to the Journey: James Baldwin's Later Fiction*
Subject: Baldwin, James, 1924-1987–Criticism and interpretation
In MARC:
600 10 $a Baldwin, James, $d 1924-1987 $v Criticism and interpretation

The aforementioned resource is not a biography of James Baldwin but a critical analysis of Baldwin's later fiction works. The addition of the free-floating subdivision *–Criticism and interpretation* to Baldwin's authorized access point is needed to emphasize this aspect of the work. There are many other free-floating subdivisions that can be assigned to personal name subject headings to highlight particular aspects of a person's life and work or materials associated with them. For example, you could assign the subdivision *–Correspondence* to a work that consists of or is about the letters exchanged between the personal name subject and someone else, like this resource:

Title: *The Letters of Mark Twain and Joseph Hopkins Twichell*
Subject: Twain, Mark, 1835-1910–Correspondence
In MARC:
600 10 $a Twain, Mark, 1835-1910 $v Correspondence

Or assign *–Parodies, imitations, etc.* to resources that imitate or parody an author's original work:

Title: *Pride and Prejudice and Zombies*
Subject: Austen, Jane, 1775-1817–Parodies, imitations, etc.
In MARC:
600 10 $a Austen, Jane, 1775-1817 $v Parodies, imitations, etc.

I recommend scanning the many free-floating subdivisions that can be assigned to personal name subject headings in the *Subject Headings Manual* H 1110 (Free-Floating Subdivisions: Names of Persons) that I also list at the end of this book, though without the additional scope notes and references to other *Subject Headings Manual* (*SHM*) instructions.

Now that we've briefly covered nonbiographical applications of personal name subject headings, let's talk about biographies and additional considerations when creating subject access to biographical materials. The main *SHM* instruction sheet applicable to these materials is *SHM* H 1330 (Biography).

Let's go over an example of a biography so you can see, step-by-step, how to assign subject headings to these works. Since we have already looked up Edgar Allan Poe's authority record, let's stick with him. (See figure 8.3.) First off, the *SHM* H 1330 (Biography) defines *biography* in this way:

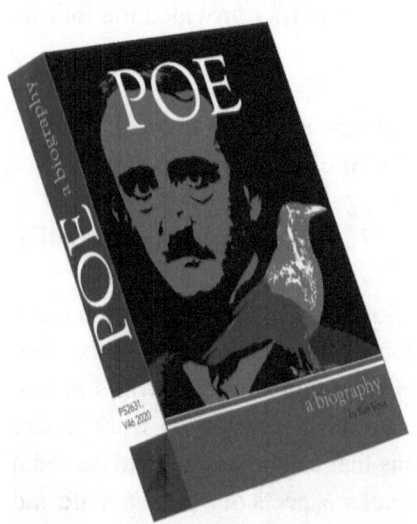

Figure 8.3. Edgar Allan Poe biography. Lauren Enjeti.

Biography (including *Autobiography*): A narrative work more than 50% of which recounts the personal aspects of the life of one or more individuals. (In the case of historical figures, particularly those from the distant past, where little is known of the personal details of their lives, the limitation of the definition to "personal aspects" does not apply.) **Personal aspects** include such details as the individual's early years, education, marriage and other personal relationships, personal habits and personality, family life, travels, personal experiences and tragedies, last years and death, etc. **Life** means a relatively large portion of the individual's life, not just a single brief incident.[1]

The definition section of *SHM* H 1330 also notes that *individual biographies* are about one individual, *collective biographies* are about two or more individuals, and *partial biographies* contain less than 50 percent biographical material.

The "general rule" at *SHM* H 1330 explains that often we should assign more than just the personal name subject heading to biographical works. The following are recommended:

- the name heading(s) for the person(s) (no more than four)
- if appropriate, a "class of persons" heading with the free-floating form subdivision *–Biography*
- if appropriate, heading(s) to bring out the person's association with a place or organization or involvement with a specific event
- topical headings, as appropriate for the work[2]

Therefore, getting back to our Edgar Allan Poe example, we should include not only Poe's name as a subject heading but also a class of persons heading and possibly other topical headings if there is a strong focus on places, events, or other topics. Perhaps a significant focus on Poe's later life in Baltimore would necessitate the inclusion of a geographic subject heading for that city, for example.

Let's begin assigning subject heading strings to the Poe biography to bring this all together.

According to *SHM* H 1330, we should assign Poe's authorized access point (name heading for the person). We already determined this earlier in the chapter when we explored Poe's authority record. The 100 field of his authority record contains his authorized access point: *Poe, Edgar Allan, 1809-1849.* If using MARC in a bibliographic record, place the name in the 600 field (personal name subject heading): 600 10 $a Poe, Edgar Allan, $d 1809-1849.

Before we move beyond this field, we need to discuss the possibility of subdivisions. In chapter 5, "MARC Coding of LCSH," the Poe example

Exception: *--***Biography** *has been established and may be used under the names of four individuals:* **Shakespeare, William, 1564-1616;** **Muḥammad, Prophet, -632;** **Jesus Christ;** *and* **Mary, Blessed Virgin, Saint***. Do not submit a proposal to establish --***Biography** *under the name of any other individual.*

Figure 8.4. SHM H 1330 biography exceptions. *Library of Congress.*

in the 600 field section contained the subdivision *–Fiction* to make it clear that the resource in question is a fiction work that features Poe as a character. Therefore, shouldn't we place *–Biography* after Poe's name to indicate we have a biography of Poe? According to *SHM* H 1330, the answer is no—do not include *–Biography* except in *very* specific circumstances, as shown in figure 8.4. *Poe, Edgar Allan, 1809-1849* it is, then.

Next, we should determine the class of persons to which Poe belongs. What does the *SHM* mean by this? *SHM* H 1100 (Free-Floating Subdivisions: Classes of Persons) states that classes of persons headings include the following:

- age and sex groups (e.g., *Youth, Women*)
- social, economic, and political categories of persons (e.g., *Poor, Political prisoners*)
- types of afflicted persons, members of particular religions (e.g., *People with mental disabilities, Catholics*)
- employees and occupational groups (e.g., *Judges, High technology industries–Employees*)

But exclude:

- social classes, e.g., *Nobility, Middle class*
- collective social groupings, e.g., *Families, Clans*
- ethnic groups and nationalities, e.g., *Hispanic Americans, Maori (New Zealand people)*

With this in mind, we should avoid adding another subject field for Poe's social class, social grouping, and ethnic or national identity and focus our attention on other categories. The *SHM* H 1330 notes that the class of persons heading "is assigned to individual biographies primarily for the benefit of public library users who are seeking biographies of a particular type of person rather than a particular individual. The heading should be selected with that in mind."[3] Since Poe is best known as an author and poet (occupational categories), these seem like the best classes of persons headings to pursue.

SHM H 1330 makes another caveat that a single class of persons heading is more desirable than multiple headings, even if a person has led a multifaceted life or career. Therefore, it is recommended that you check the records for other biographies of the person in question so that an individual is assigned class of persons headings consistently.

Other Poe biographies in WorldCat (an online union catalog that allows users to search and browse the collections of participating libraries around the world—http://worldcat.org/) use the LCSH *Authors*, and even more specifically *Authors, American*. This seems to contradict *SHM*'s earlier exclusion of ethnic groups and nationalities from the classes of persons category, but *SHM* H 1100 (Classes of Persons) goes on to say that "headings for classes of persons qualified by ethnic or national adjectival qualifiers" are fine.[4] In other words, we should not assign *American*, but qualifying *Authors* with *American* (*Authors, American*) is acceptable. According to Classification Web, *Authors, American* is a valid LCSH (see figure 8.5).

SHM H 1330 also mentions assigning *–Biography* to class of persons headings, so we definitely want to include that in our

Authors, American (May Subd Geog)
UF American authors
NT Afghan American authors
African American authors
Arab American authors
Asian American authors
Chinese American authors
Croatian American authors
Cuban American authors
Dominican American authors
Filipino American authors
German American authors

Figure 8.5. *Authors, American* entry in LCSH. *Library of Congress.*

Authors, American subject heading string to make it clear that this is biographical material. However, is there anything else we should include? *SHM* H 1155.2 (Pattern Headings: Groups of Literary Authors) suggests the inclusion of one of the following chronological subdivisions if it is appropriate (MARC subfield $y indicating a chronological subdivision):

$y Old English, ca. 450-1100
$y Middle English, 1100-1500

$y Early modern, 1500-1700
$y 18th century
$y 19th century
$y 20th century
$y 21st century

Since Poe lived during the nineteenth century, we can add that subdivision to the class of persons subject heading string (after double-checking the Free-Floating Subdivisions list, of course):

Authors, American–19th century–Biography
In MARC:
650 _0 $a Authors, American $y 19th century $v Biography

Bringing it together with the 600 field, we should assign the following subject heading strings to the Edgar Allan Poe biography:

Poe, Edgar Allan, 1809-1849
Authors, American–19th century–Biography
In MARC:
600 10 $a Poe, Edgar Allan, $d 1809-1849
650 _0 $a Authors, American $y 19th century $v Biography

As mentioned earlier, further subject heading strings should be added if certain places, events, topics, and the like are emphasized in the work.

SHM H 1330 and other rules contain further guidance on assigning classes of persons headings (H 1100), subdivisions to personal name headings (H 1110), and subdivisions for literary authors specifically (H 1155.2), and I encourage you to explore these instruction sheets. However, I want to mention one final point discussed in *SHM* H 1330.

Let's say you are describing a biography of a person where the sex or ethnicity of the person is emphasized—for example, a biography of German chancellor Angela Merkel that highlights not only her political career but also the challenges she has faced as a woman head of state. *SHM* H 1330 explains that *in addition to* assigning a more general class of persons heading, you should *also* assign a more specific class of persons heading that is qualified by sex or ethnic group. Therefore, the Angela Merkel biography should be assigned the class of persons heading *Prime ministers* and also *Women prime ministers*.

> *Merkel, Angela, 1954-*
> *Prime ministers–Germany–Biography*
> *Women prime ministers–Germany–Biography*
> In MARC:
> 600 10 $a Merkel, Angela, $d 1954-
> 650 _0 $a Prime ministers $z Germany $v Biography
> 650 _0 $a Women prime ministers $z Germany $v Biography

Since the "general rule" at *SHM* H 1330 says that it is appropriate to assign further topical or geographic subject headings, if needed, we could also assign the following after consulting LCSH:

> *Germany–Politics and government–1990-*
> In MARC:
> 651 _0 $a Germany $x Politics and government $y 1990-

Biographies, autobiographies, memoirs, and other resources that contain significant biographical material are commonplace. Therefore, it is important to assign personal name subject headings so users can find these popular resources. Personal name subject headings can be applied to other types of resources associated with a person as well, such as correspondence, criticisms of their work, and their postage stamp collections (if such works exist!). Ideally, we should all use personal name authorized access points so that these works can be found under a consistent form of someone's name, just as we do with other types of subject headings.

EXERCISES

Complete the following exercises using the Library of Congress Authorities website (http://authorities.loc.gov/) or another authority file as well as LCSH in Classification Web (or another source for finding LCSH if you cannot access Classification Web). Some will require you to consult the Free-Floating Subdivisions list. If you prefer, encode the personal name and/or subject heading string in MARC. Some questions will require you to consult the *Subject Headings Manual*.

1. List the authorized access point for each of the following using LC Authorities. If using MARC in your answer, include the coding that would be appropriate if the person is a subject heading in a bibliographic record (in other words, use the MARC 600 field):
   a. Tennis professional Serena Williams
   b. Author of the *Lord of the Rings*, J. R. R. Tolkien
   c. Former president of the United States Ulysses S. Grant
   d. Ancient queen of Egypt Cleopatra
2. Label each of the following as either the authorized access point or a variant access point for the heading for American music artist and producer Sean Combs, otherwise known as P. Diddy:
   a. Combs, Sean, 1969-
   b. Puffy, 1969-
   c. Diddy, 1969-
   d. Combs, Diddy, 1969-
   e. P. Diddy, 1969-
3. For each of the following works, assign the appropriate personal name subject heading and a free-floating subdivision to convey the subject of this work. Consult *SHM* H 1110 (Free-Floating Subdivisions: Names of Persons) to find a suitable subdivision. You may also want to consult the Free-Floating Subdivisions list in Classification Web or search for them on the LC Authorities website.
   a. A work specifically about the assassination of American president Abraham Lincoln
   b. A book of quotations by Irish poet and playwright Oscar Wilde
   c. Transcripts of interviews with American entertainer, singer, and model RuPaul
   d. A juvenile fiction work that specifically focuses on Malcolm X's wife Betty Shabazz's early life
   e. A book about American poet Emily Dickinson's close friends
4. For each of the following works, assign the appropriate personal name subject heading and at least one class of persons heading. You may also provide more specific class of persons headings if you deem them appropriate.

a. A biography of Hispanic American film actor Ramon Novarro that emphasizes his Hispanic American ethnicity
b. An autobiography of basketball player Yao Ming, who played the sport in both China and the United States
c. A memoir written by and about journalist and television producer Janet Mock that emphasizes her transgender identity and racially mixed heritage
d. A biography of American boxer Muhammad Ali for a juvenile audience (the fact that he is African American is not a significant aspect of this work)

NOTES

1. Library of Congress, "Biography—H 1330," *Subject Headings Manual*, last modified September 2013, https://www.loc.gov/aba/publications/FreeSHM/H1330.pdf.
2. Library of Congress, "Biography—H 1330."
3. Library of Congress, "Biography—H 1330."
4. Library of Congress, "Free-Floating Subdivisions: Classes of Persons—H 1100," *Subject Headings Manual*, last modified January 2020, https://www.loc.gov/aba/publications/FreeSHM/H1100.pdf.

9

Fiction

In chapter 4, "Subdivisions and Free-Floating Subdivisions," I discuss the free-floating subdivision *–Fiction* and provide several examples of the use of this subdivision in a Library of Congress subject headings (LCSH) string to convey that a work is a fictional account of a topic. In the current chapter, I want to take a closer look at fiction works because there are additional considerations beyond what we have seen with nonfiction works. I will also briefly explore the Library of Congress Children's Subject Headings, particularly useful for those who work with juvenile materials.

Just so we are on the same page, when I refer to fiction works in this chapter, I mean works that are about events, people, and places that are imaginary. The work may be *based on* a real person or event, but fiction works generally do not attempt to present a historically or topically accurate account of these subjects. J. K. Rowling's *Harry Potter and the Sorcerer's Stone*, for example, is about magic, wizards, witches, and Hogwarts School of Witchcraft and Wizardry. However, these topics are presented in the context of a fictionalized world, and therefore the subject terms assigned should reflect this fictionalized context and not imply that *Harry Potter and the Sorcerer's Stone* is a nonfiction work.

When assigning Library of Congress subject headings, it is assumed that you are applying them to nonfiction works unless you include a fiction subdivision or the heading itself asserts otherwise (such as *American fiction*—more on this in a moment). For example, examine the covers of the

Figure 9.1. Nonfiction cat supplies book. *Lauren Enjeti.*

Figure 9.2. Fiction cat supplies book. *Lauren Enjeti.*

two books shown in figures 9.1 and 9.2. Figure 9.1 shows a nonfiction work on cat supplies, and figure 9.2 shows a mystery novel about (missing) cat supplies. Though they have the same underlying topic (cat supplies), it is necessary to emphasize that one is a fictional account of the topic so that a library patron hoping to learn more about the supplies he needs to purchase for his new cat Mr. Whiskers won't be walking out the door with a cat supplies mystery novel. (Unless that was his intention!)

For this reason, we would assign the nonfiction book the following LCSH string: *Cats–Equipment and supplies*. The fiction book is assigned the same string but with the additional subdivision *–Fiction*: *Cats–Equipment and supplies–Fiction*. *–Fiction* is the subdivision assigned to nonjuvenile fiction works regardless of genre. You won't see subdivisions that convey "mystery fiction" or "romance fiction," for example. That information is usually imparted in a main heading, if it is included at all (which I will discuss in a moment). Assign the subdivision *–Juvenile fiction* to works of fiction aimed at a juvenile audience. The Library of Congress treats children and young people through high school as "juveniles" for the purposes of fiction cataloging and through ninth grade for nonfiction cataloging (see SHM H 1690—Juvenile Materials).

In LCSH, fiction is one form among many within literature, which is discussed generally in the *Subject Headings Manual* (*SHM*) H 1775 (Literature: General) and more specifically in *SHM* instructions for poetry (H 1800), drama (H 1780), legends and romances (H 1795), and elsewhere. The main *SHM* instruction document I will be referring to in this chapter is *SHM* H 1790 (Literature: Fiction), and I encourage you to follow along.

I also want to note that different library types tend to approach assigning subject headings to fiction works in different ways. For example, public and school libraries generally have more robust popular fiction collections and emphasize subject access to these collections more than academic and research libraries (such as Library of Congress). Therefore, depending on your perspective, the following discussion of Library of Congress's treatment of fiction works may be either reasonable or extremely frustrating. That is why I will provide guidance beyond the *SHM* in case you are in a position to go above and beyond Library of Congress recommendations.

In *SHM* H 1790 (Literature: Fiction), it is immediately clear that Library of Congress treats collections of fiction and individual works of fiction differently. The general rule states that "for collections of fiction, assign as many headings as necessary to bring out both the form and the topic(s)."[1] On the other hand, assigning subject headings to individual works of fiction is much more restrictive. Therefore, let's start by discussing fiction collections and then move into individual works of fiction.

FICTION COLLECTIONS—FORM HEADINGS

In *SHM* H 1425 (Collected Works and Collections), the Library of Congress refers to "collected works" and "collections" as compilations of "independent works published together in one or more volumes."[2] Collections will usually contain at least two of these independent works, wholly or in part, sometimes all by one author and sometimes by multiple authors. In this section, I will discuss form headings applied to fiction collections that include independent works written by multiple authors or one author. This is not how the *SHM* presents this information, but focusing on form headings first, then topical headings, will provide greater clarity when absorbing the *SHM* H 1790 content.

SHM H 1790 (Literature: Fiction) says to bring out the form and topic(s) when assigning subject headings to fiction collections. Back in chapter 1 of this book, I mentioned that form headings and subdivisions emphasize physical characteristics and what the resource *is* (e.g., dictionaries, diaries, maps). Let's pretend that the mystery novel about missing cat supplies from earlier is actually a collection of short stories by more than one author on that topic.

We could, of course, simply assign this work the LCSH *Fiction*, but that is not very specific—it is almost too general to be useful, especially for library collections that contain a lot of fiction works. Many of the examples Library of Congress provides in *SHM* H 1790 include the nationality of the author in the form heading, such as *American fiction–20th century* and *Short stories, American*. That, at least, is slightly more useful.

Let's assume for the sake of this example that the authors of the stories in *The Mystery of the Missing Cat Supplies* are American, and since this is a collection of mystery stories, we could assign the following LCSH: *Detective and mystery stories, American*.

If the mystery stories were by authors of different nationalities, then *Detective and mystery stories* (without the additional nationality qualifier) or the more generic *Short stories* will suffice. Library of Congress goes on to say in *SHM* H 1790 that if you assign a form heading like *Detective and mystery stories, American* that contains both form (stories) and topical (detective, mystery, American) information, you should not include topical subject headings *in addition to* the form heading. I will talk more about this disclaimer in the next section on topical subject headings.

See figure 9.3 for what the Library of Congress says about fiction collections by one author (*SHM* H 1790 2b). Note the recommendation to assign specific form headings with a topical aspect rather than nonspecific form headings. For example, if all the cat supplies mystery stories are written by Ivana Katze, then it is acceptable to assign *Detective and mystery stories, American* but not *Short stories, American*, the latter being a nonspecific form heading.

> **2. Designating the form of collections.** *(Continued)*
>
> > *b. Collections of fiction by one author.* As a general rule, assign form headings (a) if the form heading includes a topical aspect, for example, **Western stories**, or (b) if it is readily apparent from a cursory examination of the work that it comprises fiction of a highly specific form and that this form is an essential point of the collection, for example, **Allegories; Fairy tales; Radio stories; Children's stories, English**; etc.
> >
> > Do not assign nonspecific form headings to collections of fiction by one author, for example, **American fiction; Short stories, American.**

Figure 9.3. *SHM* H 1790 2b fiction collections by one author. *Library of Congress.*

However, the caveat still applies that a form heading containing topical aspects is sufficient, and further topical subject headings are not necessary. For instance, if you assign form headings with topical aspects, such as *Romance fiction*, *Sea stories*, and *Western fiction*, you do not need to assign additional topical subject headings, such as *Mermaids–Fiction* or *Cowboys–Juvenile fiction*. Furthermore, Library of Congress cautions its catalogers, "Do not attempt to assign a form heading to a collection of fiction by one author if the form is not stated on the title page or in another prominent location."[3] In other words, do not assume that a fiction collection by one author takes a certain form unless it is abundantly clear from the work itself that it is in that form (e.g., do not assign *Fairy tales* unless the work itself describes itself as a collection of fairy tales).

If you assign a form heading from LCSH and need to encode it in MARC, use the 655 field (Genre/Form) with a second indicator of zero ("0") to confirm that the term is from LCSH, despite the use of the 650 field in the *SHM* H 1790 examples, like this: 655 _0 $a Detective and mystery stories, American.

If you scroll down to the "Special Provisions for Increased Access to Fiction" section in *SHM* H 1790, specifically 3c, the Library of Congress states that form/genre headings should be placed in a 655 field, not a 650. I will discuss the "Special Provisions" section in more depth shortly.

Finally, if you assign a form or genre heading to a fiction collection (or individual fiction work, for that matter), do not add a *–Fiction* or *–Juvenile fiction* subdivision. The Library of Congress discourages the use of subdivisions with form/genre headings generally, not just the ones assigned to fiction works.

FICTION COLLECTIONS—TOPICAL SUBJECT HEADINGS

If you do not assign form headings with topical aspects to fiction collections (either by multiple people or one person), then the *SHM* says to include topical subject headings with either *–Fiction* or *–Juvenile fiction* as a form subdivision. Determine the topical focus like we have for nonfiction works in previous chapters of this book, and choose an appropriate topical subject heading from LCSH:

Horsemen and horsewomen–Fiction
Librarians–Juvenile fiction

If individual characters are emphasized in the fiction collection, assign their names as well and place *–Fiction* or *–Juvenile fiction* at the end of the string. I will discuss this in more detail in the "Special Provisions" section below. Some names can be found in LCSH, but you may need to search a name authority file, like the Library of Congress Name Authority File, for most (see chapter 8 of this book):

Holmes, Sherlock–Fiction
Potter, Harry (Fictitious character)–Juvenile fiction

Therefore, *The Mystery of the Missing Cat Supplies*, stories written by Ivana Katze and featuring her popular character Mr. Whiskers (I am totally making this up), could be assigned the following LCSH strings:

Cats–Equipment and supplies–Fiction
Mr. Whiskers (Fictitious character)–Fiction

As I mentioned earlier, if you assign a form heading like *Detective and mystery stories, American* that contains both form and topical information, the Library of Congress recommends that you should not include *additional* topical subject headings. In other words, in our cat supplies mystery collection example, we should not assign *Detective and mystery stories, American* in addition to *Cats–Equipment and supplies–Fiction*. I will say that just because Library of Congress does things one way does not mean you or your institution must follow suit. You can assign as many form or topical headings as you think are appropriate to the work. However, if you prefer to or must follow Library of Congress practice and want to include both a form heading and topical subject heading strings, then simply choose form headings that are broader and more generic, such as *American fiction* or *Short stories*. Also, if a fiction collection does not have a unified theme (each story is about a completely different topic, for example), it makes sense to assign only the form heading with or without topical aspects included in the heading. This harkens back to our discussion earlier in this book about the Library of Congress's "20 percent rule"—assign topical subject headings to works in which the topic is covered in at least 20 percent of the work.

INDIVIDUAL WORKS OF FICTION

Individual works of fiction may be created by one or more persons but contain only one story or novel. *SHM* H 1790 (Literature: Fiction) section 4 details Library of Congress practice for describing individual works of fiction. *SHM* H 1790 says explicitly that Library of Congress catalogers should "assign no form headings to individual works of adult fiction, children's fiction, or young adult fiction."[4] Instead, Library of Congress encourages assigning topical subject headings only to three types of individual works of fiction:

Biographical fiction—fiction that emphasizes a specific person or persons (e.g., *Poe, Edgar Allan, 1809-1849–Fiction*)
Historical fiction—fiction that emphasizes a specific historical event or period (e.g., *World War, 1939-1945–Fiction*)
Animal stories—fiction that emphasizes animals generally or a specific animal (e.g., *Animals–Fiction; Dogs–Fiction*)

The latter entry is good news for fans of crime-fighting cat Mr. Whiskers but not for fans of fiction works that are not biographical, historical, or animal related in some way.

If *SHM* H 1790 section 4 seems especially limiting, do not despair! As of January 2001, a section titled Special Provisions for Increased Subject Access to Fiction was added to *SHM* H 1790. According to the instructions, Library of Congress catalogers are encouraged to follow the special provisions "as internal resources permit" on "current acquisitions of American novels and novels of other English-language literatures."[5] In other words, do not expect the Library of Congress to produce records that contain robust subject heading access for all individual works of fiction, but the chances are greater now than they were before 2001 to see more topical subject headings applied to fiction works beyond those that are biographical, historical, and animal related. Nonetheless, the caveat from earlier still applies: if you are able to go beyond Library of Congress practice, do it. The next section will explore the special provisions in more detail.

SHM H 1790—SPECIAL PROVISIONS FOR INCREASED SUBJECT ACCESS TO FICTION

In Special Provisions for Increased Subject Access to Fiction (hereafter Special Provisions) General Principles section, the Library of Congress emphasizes the following categories as good candidates to use as headings applied to individual works of fiction: topic, setting, characters, form/genre. I will discuss each of these in turn.

Topical Access

Instruction #6 in Special Provisions says that topical subject headings should be assigned only if the topic is obvious from the title, dust jacket, or other conspicuous location on the resource. In other words, do not go out of your way to assign a topical subject heading if it is not explicit on the item itself. This instruction also says, "Do not assign headings for vague and general topics, such as fate, evil, belief, psychology, interpersonal relations, emotions, social customs, or community life."[6] Presumably, the Library of Congress cautions against assigning such topical subject headings to avoid the insertion of a cataloger's subjective opinion—"value judgments," as Library of Congress refers to them.[7] Then again, one seems to be on safe ground assigning, say, *Good and evil–Fiction* to a novel that clearly states on the back cover that it is about good and evil since that is in line with the first instruction about assigning topical subject headings for obvious topics. I recommend going beyond the resource itself in some circumstances. It would be unfortunate to assign *Crayons–Juvenile fiction* and not *Identity (Psychology)–Juvenile fiction* to the story about Red the crayon mentioned in chapter 2, "Basic Principles of Subject Analysis," when the description on the publisher's website clearly mentions "an identity crisis"[8] but the book itself does not.

Even though Library of Congress recommends assigning only one or two topical subject headings per resource, it is fine to consider assigning more as long as you remember to follow the principles of specificity and scope-match coverage discussed in chapter 1, "Library of Congress Subject Headings in a Nutshell." These apply to fiction works just as much as they do to nonfiction works, so try to be as specific as possible and assign topical subject headings for topics covered in at least 20 percent of the work (the Library of Congress's "20 percent rule"). Here are some examples of topical subject headings:

Interview with the Vampire by Anne Rice (a novel about vampires)
Vampires–Fiction
In MARC:
650 _0 $a Vampires $v Fiction

Watership Down by Richard Adams (a novel aimed at juveniles about a group of rabbits)
Rabbits–Juvenile fiction
In MARC:
650 _0 $a Rabbits $v Juvenile fiction

Setting

In Special Provisions instruction #5 (Setting), the Library of Congress recommends assigning subject headings to individual fiction works if the setting is a prominent feature. Setting information could include a geographic place, an event, or a time period. However, there are some caveats. First, avoid assigning subject headings or subdivisions related to time period if the fiction work is set during the same time period in which it was written. For example, do not include *–20th century* in a subject heading string describing a fiction work written during the twentieth century. This also applies to geographic setting. If the geographic setting of a book is the same as where the author currently lives, do not include the geographic aspect in the subject heading string. Finally, if an imaginary place or organization features prominently in *at least* three works, then it is fine to include a subject heading for it. Otherwise, do not. Here are some examples of individual fiction works where setting features prominently:

Outlander by Diana Gabaldon (an Englishwoman travels back in time to eighteenth-century Scotland)
Time travel–Fiction
Jacobite Rebellion, 1745-1746–Fiction
Scotland–History–18th century–Fiction

In MARC:

650 _0 $a Time travel $v Fiction
650 _0 $a Jacobite Rebellion, 1745-1746 $v Fiction
651 _0 $a Scotland $x History $y 18th century $v Fiction

The War that Saved My Life by Kimberly Brubaker Bradley (a brother and sister are sent to live outside of London during World War II)
Children with disabilities–Juvenile fiction
Brothers and sisters–Juvenile fiction
World War, 1939-1945–Evacuation of civilians–Great Britain–Juvenile fiction

In MARC:

650 _0 $a Children with disabilities $v Juvenile fiction
650 _0 $a Brothers and sisters $v Juvenile fiction
650 _0 $a World War, 1939-1945 $x Evacuation of civilians $z Great Britain $v Juvenile fiction

Ninth Ward by Jewell Parker Rhodes (a girl and her family from the Ninth Ward neighborhood in New Orleans, Louisiana, are caught in Hurricane Katrina in 2005)
Survival–Juvenile fiction
Hurricane Katrina, 2005–Juvenile fiction
Ninth Ward (New Orleans, La.)–Juvenile fiction

In MARC:

650_0 $a Survival $v Juvenile fiction
650 _0 $a Hurricane Katrina, 2005 $v Juvenile fiction
651 _0 $a Ninth Ward (New Orleans, La.) $v Juvenile fiction

Characters

Instruction #4 (Characters) in the Special Provisions provides guidance on assigning character names and class of persons subject headings associated with a character. The Library of Congress has separate instructions for characters created by an author and characters *not* created by an author. Section 4a notes that works with main characters that are real people, legendary, or not originally invented by the author of the work should be assigned as subject headings with *–Fiction* or *–Juvenile fiction* as a subdivision. Examples include a fiction novel with Edgar Allan Poe as a main character and British legendary character Sweeney Todd.

Conversely, subject headings for main characters created by the author of a work should not be assigned unless they feature prominently in at least three works. Therefore, it is fine to assign the subject heading *Thomas, Odd (Fictitious character)* to the Odd Thomas series of books created by Dean Koontz since there are more than three books in that series with him as a main character. However, you should not assign character subject headings for the Dean Koontz books where the main character (assuming it is created by Koontz) appears in fewer than three of his books. The same rule applies to characters who may appear in only one or two works by the author who created them but have taken on a life of their own beyond the original work. For instance, the character Dorian Gray appeared only in Oscar Wilde's novel *The Picture of Dorian Gray* but is featured in multiple books and films written by others and should be added as a subject heading if he is a main character in these works. (See figure 9.4.)

In addition to assigning the character name as a subject heading, class of persons headings can be applied "if that class of persons is established and is likely to be sought by the typical public library user, for example, women detectives."[9] You should follow the same advice from chapter 8,

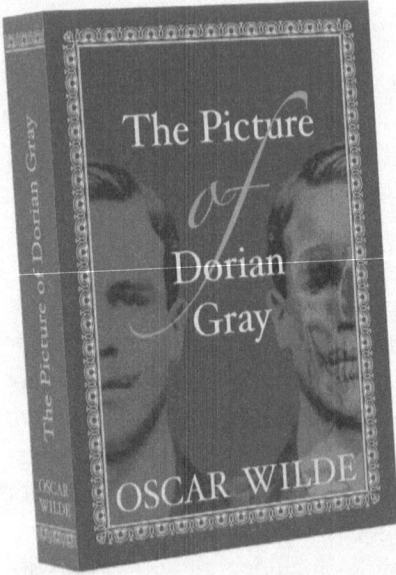

Figure 9.4. *The Picture of Dorian Gray by Oscar Wilde. Lauren Enjeti.*

"Personal Name Subject Headings and Biographies," and assign class of persons headings only if the subject's sex/gender, race, or ethnic class features prominently in the work. For example, *The Tubman Command*, a novel by Elizabeth Cobbs, has as a main character Harriet Tubman, a real African American woman and former slave who helped many other slaves escape their bondage. To this work we should assign Harriet Tubman's name plus the *–Fiction* subdivision as well as a class of persons heading for *African American women* or perhaps *African American women abolitionists* (plus the *–Fiction* subdivision) since the fact that she is an African American and a woman is emphasized in the work.

Here are some further examples of individual fiction works where characters feature prominently:

> *Circe: A Novel* by Madeline Miller (about the Greek mythological figure Circe)
> *Circe (Mythological character)–Fiction*
> *Witches–Fiction*

In MARC:

600 00 $a Circe (Mythological character) $v Fiction
650 _0 $a Witches $v Fiction

> *The Adventures of Captain Underpants: An Epic Novel* by Dav Pilkey (the adventures of the diapered superhero Captain Underpants)
> *Captain Underpants (Fictitious character)–Juvenile fiction*

School principals–Juvenile fiction
Heroes–Juvenile fiction

In MARC:

600 00 $a Captain Underpants (Fictitious character) $v Juvenile fiction
650 _0 $a School principals $v Juvenile fiction
650 _0 $a Heroes $v Juvenile fiction

Form/Genre

Finally, Special Provisions instruction #3 (Form and Genre Headings) reviews when and how to apply form and genre headings to individual works of fiction. We have already discussed the use of form headings earlier in this chapter, but this section will provide further guidance. The first bit of information that differs from what was discussed earlier in *SHM* H 1790 is the recommendation at 3a to use the second edition of the *Guidelines on Subject Access to Individual Works of Fiction, Drama, Etc. (GSAFD)*. The *GSAFD* is a list created by the American Library Association that is "a recommendation for national standard practice in the provision of genre and subject access to individual works of fiction, drama, poetry, humor, and folklore in all formats."[10] The second (and most recent) edition was released in the year 2000, and there is no indication that further editions are forthcoming. References to the *GSAFD* in the *Subject Headings Manual* will likely be fewer in future revisions now that the Library of Congress has invested more time and resources into its own *Library of Congress Genre/Form Terms for Library and Archival Materials (LCGFT)*, which I will discuss in a moment. Regardless, it is worth exploring *GSAFD* since it is a pretty straightforward and succinct list that has been around longer than *LCGFT*. You can search or browse *GSAFD* by going to this website, which does not require a subscription: http://experimental.worldcat.org/gsafd/.

GSAFD headings include fiction genres such as *Adventure fiction*, *Ghost stories*, and *Medical novels*. Special Provisions 3a recommends the use of unqualified genre headings from LCSH if you cannot locate an appropriate heading in *GSAFD* as well as assigning one or two headings at most to capture the main genre(s) of the resource.

In 3b, it is noted that when assigned to individual works of fiction, form/genre headings should be as specific as possible—avoid more general headings such as *Fiction* or *Short Stories*. However, "do not include adjectival qualifiers or subdivisions that show the language of the work or that reflect the characteristics of the author, such as nationality, religion, sex, ethnic background."[11] In other words, you should not assign headings such as *Ghost stories, Mexican*, which is a valid LCSH, to an individual Mexican ghost story due to the inclusion of a nationality. However, it is acceptable to assign such headings to fiction collections.

Special Provisions 3c discusses the MARC coding of *GSAFD* headings. Use MARC field 655 (genre/form headings) with a second indicator of "7" (source specified in subfield $2), and place $2 gsafd at the end of the field to state that the term is from the *GSAFD*. Here is an example: 655 _7 $a Medical novels. $2 gsafd.

Though not mentioned in *SHM* H 1790, the LCGFT is another form/genre list that is much more robust than *GSAFD* and updated more recently and regularly. You can access the *LCGFT* through Classification Web (LC Genre/Form Terms), and it is also available in PDFs on the Library of Congress's website (https://www.loc.gov/aba/publications/FreeLCGFT/freelcgft.html) and the LC Authorities website (https://authorities.loc.gov/).

The *LCGFT* contains many form/genre headings that apply to resources beyond fiction works, such as films, sound recordings, and cartographic materials. Fiction form/genre headings are not as plentiful as headings for other types of materials. Nonetheless, *LCGFT* can be helpful for supplementing the form/genre options provided by LCSH and *GSAFD*. There is a *Library of Congress Genre/Form Terms Manual* that you can find on the Library of Congress website I mentioned earlier. The manual's instruction sheet J 235 for Literature makes only one recommendation for fiction works: "assign a term that indicates the length of the resource when it is readily apparent (e.g., Novels; Novellas; Short stories; Flash fiction)."[12] See figure 9.5.

J 235 also mentions instruction sheet J 110, which discusses assigning genre/form terms. This document largely echoes what we have seen elsewhere in the *Subject Headings Manual*, but there is additional information that is worth noting. First of all, J 110 reminds us that *LCGFT* does not (and will not) contain a form/genre term that fits every resource, especially if multiple forms and genres are involved. Instead, broader terms should be applied to situations when multiple forms and genres apply. For example, it is not uncommon to find a romance novel that also has science-fiction genre elements or a fantasy fiction work that is also a mystery. In these cases, understand that there will not be one genre heading that encompasses all aspects—separate headings should be assigned. For instance, the romance novel that is also within the science-fiction genre could be assigned the following three form/genre headings: *Romance fiction*, *Science fiction*, and *Novels*.

Figure 9.5. *A Starship Named Desire*, science-fiction/romance novel. *Lauren Enjeti*

Lastly, I mentioned this earlier, but it bears repeating: you cannot subdivide form/genre headings. This is the case for all form/genre headings assigned to nonfiction and fiction works, not just for *LCGFT* or *GSAFD*. If you feel the urge to subdivide that form/genre heading by time period or geographic place, resist the temptation!

Like *GSAFD*, use MARC field 655, second indicator "7" for *LCGFT* terms, but put *$2 lcgft* at the end of the field to state that the term is from the *LCGFT*: 655 _7 $a Fantasy fiction. $2 lcgft.

LIBRARY OF CONGRESS CHILDREN'S SUBJECT HEADINGS

All the instructions discussed thus far apply equally to adult and juvenile fiction materials, but school and public library users may benefit from additional subject access through the Library of Congress Children's Subject Headings (CSH). Since the focus of this book is LCSH, I won't go into too much detail about the CSH, but it is useful to have a basic understanding of how to find and apply these headings if you work with children's materials, whether fiction or nonfiction.

The CSH terms were developed by the Library of Congress as part of their Children's and Young Adults' Cataloging (CYAC) program.[13] Formerly called the Annotated Card program, CYAC focuses on providing subject access to fiction English-language juvenile materials. According to the CYAC website,[14] the following types of materials are within the scope of the program:

- collections and single works of fiction for children and young adults
- juvenile graphic novels
- juvenile novels in verse
- original and traditional fairy tales
- folklore
- fables
- classical nursery rhymes (e.g., Mother Goose)
- stories in rhyme
- song lyrics presented in a picture-book format
- fiction about realistic animals
- bilingual and polyglot fiction for children and young adults
- fiction for children and young adults presented in or featuring Braille or sign language

The CSH can be found in Classification Web (LC Children's Subject Headings) and the LC Authorities website: https://authorities.loc.gov/. I will not cover all the features of CSH or how it differs from LCSH. Instead, here are some key aspects of CSH to keep in mind:

- The CSH is not a comprehensive list of terms—it supplements LCSH. Therefore, if you cannot find the term you need in the CSH, default to the LCSH term. For example, LCSH has a heading for *Sleepwalking*, but the CSH does not.
- Since materials in a juvenile collection are assumed to be for children, CSH does not often include "juvenile" or "children" (and their variations) in the headings or subdivisions. For example, a fiction book about children's parties written for children would be assigned *Children's parties* in LCSH but only *Parties* in CSH. In addition, we

would use the subdivision *–Fiction* and not *–Juvenile fiction*. LCSH: *Children's parties–Juvenile fiction*. CSH: *Parties–Fiction*.
- The CSH also has more tolerance for assigning broader *and* narrower terms to the same resource because this is thought to be more useful for young people when they are searching the catalog. For example, assign *Sports–Fiction* in addition to the more specific *Baseball–Fiction* to a juvenile fiction work about baseball.

I encourage you to read through CYAC's page on the CSH for further information about and guidance on assigning CSH: https://www.loc.gov/aba/cyac/childsubjhead.html. Use the same MARC coding for CSH as we have discussed previously, but you must place "1" in the second indicator spot instead of "0" to indicate that you are using the CSH:

650 _1 $a Parties $v Fiction
650 _1 $a Sports $v Fiction

This chapter on subject access to fiction works provided an overview of *Subject Headings Manual* guidance on what to assign to fiction collections and individual works of fiction. The instructions can be confusing, but I will tell you what I tell my students: focus on including the subject/form/genre headings that you think will be most helpful to people trying to *find* what you are describing. If you need to enhance a catalog record with more robust subject terms in your local catalog in order to achieve that goal, do your best to make that happen.

EXERCISES

In this section of exercises, answer the following questions using information found in this chapter and the applicable instructions in the *Subject Headings Manual*.

1. Using LCSH (not CSH), determine if *–Fiction* or *–Juvenile fiction* is most appropriate as a form subdivision for subject headings applied to fiction works aimed at each of the following target audiences:
   a. First graders

b. High school seniors
   c. Seventh graders
   d. College freshmen
2. For each of the form headings below, use *SHM* H 1790 to determine if a topical heading is needed when cataloging a fiction collection by one or more authors:
   a. Short stories
   b. Erotic stories
   c. Science fiction, Canadian
   d. Bildungsromans
   e. Diary fiction
   f. Beat fiction
3. In which MARC field should form headings be encoded?
4. According to *SHM* H 1790, section 4, which of the following headings should be applied to individual works of fiction?
   a. Form headings
   b. Topical headings that express the biographical aspects of the work
   c. Topical headings that express the psychological aspects of the work
   d. Topical headings that express the historical aspects of the work
5. Which section of *SHM* H 1790 was added in 2001 that encouraged LC catalogers to increase subject access to works of fiction? What works of fiction are included in its scope? Which categories of headings may be appropriate to apply to works covered in this section?
6. Identify and correct the errors in the cataloging for individual works of fiction assigned the headings in each of the following scenarios:
   a. A fantastical retelling of the life of Chinese philosopher Confucius: *Confucius* and *Fantasy fiction*
   b. A romance between two electricians: *Electricians–Fiction, Fiction,* and *Romance fiction*
   c. A mystery that involves two office employees, a man and a woman, who work together: *Man-woman relationships–Fiction, Clerks–Fiction,* and *Detective and mystery stories*
   d. A contemporary novel about scientists in Zimbabwe written by a Namibian author in English: *Scientists–Zimbabwe–Fiction* and *Namibian fiction (English)–21st century*

7. In the remaining exercises, assign Library of Congress subject headings and subdivisions as well as genre/form headings (if needed) to the works described below. Use Classification Web (or another source for finding LCSH if you cannot access Classification Web), the *Guidelines on Subject Access to Individual Works of Fiction, Drama, Etc.*, and/or *Library of Congress Genre/Form Terms for Library and Archival Materials*. If you prefer, encode your answers in MARC.
   a. A juvenile fiction work on the extinction of dinosaurs
   b. A collection of environmental fiction short stories
   c. A collection of fiction by various Swedish authors, primarily about European football and fans of the sport (use a broad, nontopical form heading)
   d. A choose-your-own-story novel (for a juvenile audience) about animal robots and children who are inventors
   e. A fiction book within the "steampunk" genre that features a cursed amulet and romance

NOTES

1. Library of Congress, "Literature: Fiction—H 1790," *Subject Headings Manual*, last modified November 2015, https://www.loc.gov/aba/publications/FreeSHM/H1790.pdf (Section 1, page 1).

2. Library of Congress, "Collected Works and Collections—H 1425," *Subject Headings Manual*, last modified June 2013, https://www.loc.gov/aba/publications/FreeSHM/H1425.pdf.

3. Library of Congress, "Literature: Fiction—H 1790," section 5, 3.

4. Library of Congress, "Literature: Fiction—H 1790," section 4, 3.

5. Library of Congress, "Literature: Fiction—H 1790," Special Provisions, 5.

6. Library of Congress, "Literature: Fiction—H 1790," Special Provisions, 8.

7. Library of Congress, "Literature: Fiction—H 1790," section 5, 3.

8. "Red: A Crayon's Story," HarperCollins, accessed November 28, 2020, https://www.harpercollins.com/products/red-michael-hall?variant=32129318649890.

9. Library of Congress, "Literature: Fiction—H 1790," Special Provisions, 7.

10. "Search/Browse GSAFD," OCLC, accessed November 28, 2020, http://experimental.worldcat.org/gsafd/.

11. Library of Congress, "Literature: Fiction—H 1790," Special Provisions, 6.

12. Library of Congress, "Literature: J 235," *Library of Congress Genre/Form Terms PDF Files*, last modified January 2016, https://www.loc.gov/aba/publications/FreeLCGFT/J235.pdf.

13. Library of Congress, "About the Program," *Children's and Young Adults' Cataloging Program (CYAC)*, last modified April 13, 2015, https://www.loc.gov/aba/cyac/about.html.

14. Library of Congress, "About the Program."

10

Conclusion and LCSH Resources

You've made it to the end of this condensed exploration of Library of Congress subject headings (LCSH). Congratulations! I hope you now feel more confident in your ability to locate and assign Library of Congress subject headings; subdivisions; personal name subject headings; geographic subject headings; and topical, form, and genre headings to fiction works. Gaining proficiency in LCSH takes time and experience, so if you have been skipping the end-of-chapter exercises, head back to them and practice, practice, practice! The answers to all exercises follow this chapter.

Also, keep in mind that it is quite helpful to consult records in other catalogs and WorldCat.org to see what subject headings others have assigned to resources on a similar topic. Why start from scratch when you have a wealth of cataloging knowledge in various catalogs at your disposal? For example, if you are struggling with assigning subject headings on the social customs of women in ancient Greece, locating works on a similar topic can give you a head start. However, a word of caution: it is not uncommon for catalog records to contain incorrect or outdated subject headings and subdivisions. Therefore, you should always remain skeptical and double-check LCSH, the Free-Floating Subdivisions list, and the *Subject Headings Manual* before using the subject terms you find in other catalogs.

Finally, since I mentioned quite a few resources throughout this book, I thought it would be helpful to have an easy-to-find reference list here so you do not have to flip through this whole book to find one website. In addition, I included at the end of the list some books about LCSH that I recommend if you need a deeper dive into the subject.

REFERENCES

Children's Subject Headings (CSH) Information (https://www.loc.gov/aba/cyac/childsubjhead.html). Information on the Library of Congress's website about the Children's Subject Headings list.

Guidelines on Subject Access to Individual Works of Fiction, Drama, Etc. (*GSAFD*) (http://experimental.worldcat.org/gsafd/). Provides searching and browsing access to the *GSAFD*.

Library of Congress. Classification Web (https://classweb.org/). A subscription-based resource that contains not only the Library of Congress subject headings and Free-Floating Subdivisions lists but also other cataloging resources, such as the Library of Congress classification (LCC) schedules and tables and the Library of Congress Children's Subject Headings (CSH). Also contains the Bibliographic Correlations tool that can provide Library of Congress subject headings that correspond to specific Dewey Decimal classification numbers and LCC numbers.

Library of Congress. PDFs of Library of Congress Subject Headings (https://www.loc.gov/aba/cataloging/subject/). PDFs of LCSH (and other resources) that are free to access but lack the functionality of LCSH in Classification Web.

Library of Congress. *Subject Headings Manual* (*SHM*) (https://www.loc.gov/aba/publications/FreeSHM/freeshm.html). Library of Congress's guide to LCSH. It contains information on how to create and assign LCSH and subdivisions, covering a wide variety of resources and topics. You can also access *SHM* through Cataloger's Desktop (https://desktop.loc.gov/) if your institution has a subscription to it.

Library of Congress Authorities (http://authorities.loc.gov/). Free, web-based authority file containing authority records for names, subjects, and titles.

Library of Congress Genre/Form Terms (*LCGFT*) (https://www.loc.gov/aba/publications/FreeLCGFT/freelcgft.html). Provides information about and guidance for assigning *LCGFT* as well as a PDF list of *LCGFT*.

Library of Congress Linked Data Service (http://id.loc.gov/). Website that contains authority information for names, subjects, titles, and much more. Does not use MARC coding.

Library of Congress MARC21 Format for Bibliographic Data (http://www.loc.gov/marc/bibliographic/). Provides information about and usage instructions for Library of Congress MARC21 for bibliographic data for the creation of bibliographic records in a library catalog.

Library of Congress MARC21 Format for Authority Data (http://www.loc.gov/marc/authority/). Provides information about and usage instructions for Library of Congress MARC21 for authority data found in authority records like you would find on the LC Authorities website.

OCLC Bibliographic Formats and Standards (https://www.oclc.org/bibformats/en.html). Provides information about and usage instructions for OCLC MARC for the creation of bibliographic records in a library catalog.

OCLC Connexion Browser (http://connexion.oclc.org/). Subscription-based program from OCLC that, among other features, includes the OCLC WorldCat authority file containing authority records for names, subjects, and titles.

TRAINING MATERIALS AND BOOKS ABOUT LCSH

Basic Subject Cataloging Using LCSH: Trainee's Manual (from ALCTS and the PCC) (https://www.loc.gov/catworkshop/courses/basicsubject/pdf/lcsh-trnee-manual.pdf). A free and helpful guide to LCSH with exercises put together by the Program for Cooperative Cataloging (PCC) and the Association for Library Collections and Technical Services (ALCTS).

Broughton, Vanda. *Essential Library of Congress Subject Headings* (New York: Neal-Schuman, 2012). Another comprehensive look at LCSH and its application. Also includes a few exercises.

Cataloging Lab (http://cataloginglab.org/). A collaborative project that assists those seeking to change or add to LCSH and other standards as well.

Chan, Lois Mai. *Library of Congress Subject Headings: Principles and Application* (Westport, CT: Libraries Unlimited, 2005). Comprehensive coverage of the history and principles of LCSH as well as the methods of assigning LCSH and subdivisions.

Intermediate LC Subject Headings, II (from ALCTS; presenter Bobby Bothmann) (http://www.ala.org/alcts/confevents/upcoming/webinar/030317). A free recorded webinar from 2017 that builds on the introductory webinar listed above. There is also free access to the presentation slides.

Introduction to LC Subject Headings, I (from ALCTS; presenter Bobby Bothmann) (http://www.ala.org/alcts/confevents/upcoming/webinar/030117). A free recorded webinar from 2017 on the basics of LCSH. There is also free access to the presentation slides.

Library of Congress Subject Headings: Online Training (from the Library of Congress) (https://loc.gov/catworkshop/lcsh/index.html). A free and helpful guide to LCSH with exercises put together by the Library of Congress.

BOOKS ON BIAS IN LCSH (CHAPTER 1)

Adler, Melissa. *Cruising the Library: Perversities in the Organization of Knowledge* (New York: Fordham University Press, 2017).

Berman, Sanford. *Prejudices and Antipathies: A Tract on the LC Subject Heads Concerning People* (Jefferson, NC: McFarland, 1993). http://www.sanfordberman.org/prejant.htm.

Olson, Hope A. *The Power to Name: Locating the Limits of Subject Representation in Libraries* (Norwell, MA: Kluwer Academic, 2002).

Appendix A
Answers to End-of-Chapter Exercises

CHAPTER 1

1. What does the Library of Congress primarily rely on to determine which terms should be included in LCSH? **ANSWER:** Literary warrant.
2. Name two places on the web where you can find LCSH. **ANSWER:** Your answers could include any of the following: Classification Web (https://classweb.org/), Library of Congress's Authorities website (http://authorities.loc.gov/), Library of Congress's linked data service (http://id.loc.gov/), an OCLC product such as Connexion, and the PDFs on Library of Congress's website (https://www.loc.gov/aba/cataloging/subject/).
3. Read each explanation below, and identify the type of relationship described as an equivalence relationship, a hierarchical relationship, or an associative relationship.
    a. In LCSH, *Solar system* is a narrower term under *Milky Way* but is broader than *Planets*. What type of relationship do these terms have? **ANSWER:** Hierarchical.
    b. *Buckets* and *pails* are considered synonyms in LCSH. What type of relationship do these terms have? **ANSWER:** Equivalence.
    c. The LCSH *Folklore* has several related terms, such as *Mythology* and *Storytelling*, that do not have the same meaning and are not

considered broader or narrower terms. What type of relationship do these terms have? **ANSWER:** Associative.
4. Using the principle of specificity and the LCSH hierarchy (economics → economic policy → government spending policy → employment subsidies), answer the following questions:
   a. Is it appropriate to assign *Economics* to a general work on economic policy? Explain. **ANSWER:** No. Assign *Economic policy* because it is most specific to the topic of the work.
   b. Is it appropriate to assign *Employment subsidies* to a general work on government spending policy that discusses employment subsidies among other government spending policies? Explain. **ANSWER:** No. Not enough detail given to say otherwise.
   c. Is it appropriate to assign *Economic policy* to a general work on economic policy? Explain. **ANSWER:** Yes. The heading is at the appropriate level of specificity given the topic of the work.
5. Use the principle of scope-match and the above *Economics* hierarchy to determine which response (assign the headings for each type of policy or assign the general topic heading *Economic policy*) is the most appropriate to the scenarios provided in a and b. Explain your choice.
   a. A work on economic policy comprised of three equal parts that cover government spending policy, labor policy, and monetary policy (all types of economic policy). **ANSWER:** Assign the headings for each type of policy. Since all three topics are covered equally and are the primary topics of the work, it is fine to assign subject headings for all three topics.
   b. A work on economic policy with twelve chapters each covering a different type of policy. **ANSWER:** Assign the general topic heading *Economic policy*. Each type of policy is not covered in at least 20 percent of the work.

CHAPTER 2

1. What does SLAM stand for? What does SLAM help you do? **ANSWER:** SLAM stands for **S**can, **L**ook for, **A**sk yourself, and **M**entally compose. SLAM helps with the subject analysis process.

2. Name two sources of information that you should consult during the first step of the SLAM method. **ANSWER:** Any two of the following: title page (or title screen, card, etc.), introduction, preface, table of contents, front and back cover/dust jacket (or front and back of the container), bibliography and index, any other documentation that is on or comes with the resource, Cataloging-in-Publication (CIP) data.
3. What aspects of a resource should you consider beyond those examined in the first step of the SLAM method when identifying keywords or phrases that describe what the work is about? **ANSWER:** Consider the author's intent, the intended audience, and any special viewpoint presented.
4. What two actions typically occur during the subject analysis process, according to library and information science literature? **ANSWER:** Conceptual analysis and translation.
5. What is it called when single-concept terms are combined to form complex subjects *prior* to the user's search of a system? **ANSWER:** Precoordination.
6. Besides aboutness, what else might be important to identify in the subject analysis process? **ANSWER:** Is-ness information, such as form, as well as genre information.

CHAPTER 3

1. What is the LCSH for book owners? **ANSWER:** *Book collectors.*
2. What is the LCSH for prehistoric animals? **ANSWER:** *Animals, Fossil.*
3. What is the LCSH for boats? **ANSWER:** *Boats and boating.*
4. What is the LCSH for futility? **ANSWER:** *Frustration.*
5. What is the BT (broader term) associated with the LCSH *Unicorns*? **ANSWER:** *Animals, Mythical.*
6. What is the RT (related term) associated with the LCSH *Fortune-telling by cards*? **ANSWER:** *Divination cards.*
7. What are the NTs (narrower terms) associated with *Imaginary vehicles*? **ANSWER:** *Imaginary space vehicles* and *Imaginary submarines.*

8. What are the UF (used for) headings associated with *Alchemy*? **ANSWER:** *Metals, Transmutation of*; *Philosophers' egg*; *Philosophers' stone*; *Stone, Philosophers'*; and *Transmutation of metals*.
9. What does the SA (see also) note say at LCSH *Clothing and dress*? **ANSWER:** SA subdivision *Clothing* under names of individual persons and families and under classes of persons and ethnic groups.
10. Can the LCSH *Desserts* be subdivided geographically? What about the LCSH *Desserts in art*? **ANSWER:** Yes to the first question. No to the second. *Desserts* has *(May Subd Geog)* after it and *Desserts in art* has *(Not Subd Geog)*.

CHAPTER 4

1. A work about collecting snow globes. **ANSWER:** *Snowdomes–Collectors and collecting*.
2. A work about the grooming of sheep. **ANSWER:** *Sheep–Grooming*.
3. A work about museums in France. **ANSWER:** *Museums–France*.
4. A work about construction industry employees. **ANSWER:** *Construction industry–Employees*.
5. A work of fiction about an only child that is meant for a juvenile audience. **ANSWER:** *Only child–Juvenile fiction*.
6. A work about medical care in the United States. **ANSWER:** *Medical care–United States*.
7. A work on the fading of the color of corn. **ANSWER:** *Corn–Color–Fading*.
8. A work on dog parties of the twenty-first century. **ANSWER:** *Parties for dogs* or *Parties for dogs–History–21st century*. If you search for "dog parties" in LCSH, it will tell you to use *Parties for dogs*. The valid subdivision for the time period *twenty-first century* is *–21st century*, a free-floating subdivision. However, the scope note for *–21st century* says this: "Use as a chronological subdivision under headings for art and art forms of all nations, regions, and ethnic groups. Also use under individual languages and groups of languages, groups of literary authors, individual literatures, including drama, and forms and types of musical compositions." *Parties*

for dogs does not fit the scope of this subdivision, so it cannot be used. Therefore, you should have *Parties for dogs* or, if we really need to have the time period included, the Free-Floating Subdivisions list says that *–History–21st century* is valid after any topical heading: *Parties for dogs–History–21st century*.
9. A book of poetry that is primarily about the size of raindrops. **ANSWER:** *Raindrops–Size–Poetry*.
10. A dictionary of twentieth-century modernist art. **ANSWER:** *Modernism (Art)–20th century–Dictionaries*.

CHAPTER 5

1. A work on the history of butter carving. **ANSWER:**

Butter sculpture–History
650 _0 $a Butter sculpture $x History

2. A work on the identification of the mountain lion. **ANSWER:**

Puma–Identification
650 _0 $a Puma $v Identification

Make sure you use $v (form) instead of $x (topical) because the Free-Floating Subdivisions list states at the entry for *–Identification*: use as a form subdivision under individual animals and groups of animals, individual plants and groups of plants, and types of objects for works presenting the characteristics of a group for the purpose of determining the names of its members.

3. A work on pet food recipes. **ANSWER:**

Pets–Feeding and feeds–Recipes
650 _0 $a Pets $x Feeding and feeds $v Recipes

4. A work about the places frequented by American singer and actress Cher (her authorized access point is Cher, 1946-). **ANSWER:**

Cher, 1946- –Homes and haunts
600 00 $a Cher, 1946- $x Homes and haunts

5. A work about pillage during the First World War. **ANSWER:**

World War, 1914-1918–Destruction and pillage
650 _0 $a World War, 1914-1918 $x Destruction and pillage

6. A manual on the prevention of attacks by bears. **ANSWER:**

Bear attacks–Prevention–Handbooks, manuals, etc.
650 _0 $a Bear attacks $x Prevention $v Handbooks, manuals, etc.

7. A work of fiction about the use of bees in war. **ANSWER:**

Bees–War use–Fiction
650 _0 $a Bees $x War use $v Fiction

8. A board book for young children. **ANSWER:**

Board books
655 _0 $a Board books

9. A work about games for children. **ANSWER:**

Games
650 _0 $a Games

LCSH says to use *Games* for the topic of games for children. You cannot use *Children's games* nor can you use the Free-Floating Subdivision *–Games* because it can be used only under ethnic groups.

10. A work about the social life and customs in New York City during the American colonial period. The authorized access point for New York City is New York (N.Y.). **ANSWER:**

New York (N.Y.)–Social life and customs–To 1775
651 _0 $a New York (N.Y.) $x Social life and customs $y To 1775

CHAPTER 6

1. What is the *SHM* instruction number associated with guidance on the following topics or type of materials?
   a. Songs and music. **ANSWER:** H 2075.
   b. Artistic photography. **ANSWER:** H 1255.
   c. Government publications. **ANSWER:** H 1643.
   d. Emigration and immigration. **ANSWER:** H 1581.
   e. Translations. **ANSWER:** H 2220.
2. Use H 0180 (Assigning and Constructing Subject Headings) to answer the following questions:
   a. According to section 12 (Concepts in Titles), if the title of the work is general but the actual content of the work is specific, what heading(s) should you assign to the work? **ANSWER:** Headings for the specific topic(s).
   b. According to section 4 (Specificity), when is it appropriate to assign a broader or more general heading to a work about a more specific topic? **ANSWER:** According to the *SHM*, "Assign a heading that is broader or more general than the topic that it is intended to cover only when it is not possible to establish a precise heading, when an array of headings is needed to express the topic, or when the assignment of a more general heading is called for by special instructions in the Subject Headings Manual."
   c. If I am cataloging a work titled *The Best Tea Making Paraphernalia: Balls, Bowls, and Cozies*, do I assign to this work the LCSH *Tea making paraphernalia*? **ANSWER:** No. According to *SHM* H 0180 section 8 (Rule of Three), if a broader topic contains more than three subtopics, but only two or three of the subtopics are discussed in a work, then assign subject headings

for the subtopics and not the broader topic. Therefore, we should assign *Tea balls*, *Tea bowls*, and *Tea cozies* to *The Best Tea Making Paraphernalia: Balls, Bowls, and Cozies* book.
d. You are cataloging a work titled *Grandfathers and Grandmothers: Guidance on Your New Family Role*. Is it appropriate to assign the headings *Grandmothers–Family relationships* and *Grandfathers–Family relationships* to this work? **ANSWER:** No. Since the broader heading *Grandparents* includes only *Grandmothers and Grandfathers*, *SHM* 0180 section 7 (Two or Three Related Headings) says to assign one broad heading rather than the two narrower headings.
3. What is/are the pattern heading(s) for the following topics:
   a. Animals. **ANSWER:** *Fishes; Cattle.*
   b. Plants and crops. **ANSWER:** *Corn.*
   c. Legal topics. **ANSWER:** *Labor Laws and Legislation.*
   d. Religions. **ANSWER:** *Buddhism.*
4. Identify the *SHM* rule that applies to the creation of subject headings related to specific events, and answer the following questions, providing the section numbers that led to your answer:
   a. Should *State Fair of Texas* be established as a name heading or a subject heading? **ANSWER:** Name heading. *SHM* 1592 (Events) section 2.
   b. Should *Riots* be established as a name heading or a subject heading? **ANSWER:** Subject heading. *SHM* 1592 (Events) section 1.
   c. If you are cataloging a book about the Zoot Suit Riots that occurred in Los Angeles, California, in 1943, how would you formulate that heading? **ANSWER:**

[name of event], [name of jurisdiction or locality], [date or date span]
Zoot Suit Riots, Los Angeles, Calif., 1943.
SHM 1592 (Events) section 4

5. Identify the *SHM* rule that applies to pictorial works, and answer the following questions, providing the section numbers that led to your answer.
   a. I am cataloging a book about rainbows that consists entirely of pictures of rainbows. Is this subject heading string sufficient?

Rainbows–Pictorial works. **ANSWER:** Yes. According to *SHM* H 1935 (Pictorial Works) section 1a, if a work consists entirely of pictures or contains mostly pictures with very little text, then assign a subject heading for the main topic and subdivide it with *–Pictorial works.*
  b. I am cataloging a book about rainbows that contains a substantial amount of text, but it also contains a lot of pictures (at least 50 percent of the book), and special credit is given to the illutrator. Is this subject heading string sufficient? *Rainbows–Pictorial works.* **ANSWER:** No. According to *SHM* H 1935 (Pictorial Works) section 1b, if a work has text accompanied by illustrations in at least 50 percent of the work, you should assign not only the main subject heading but also an additional subject heading string that includes *–Pictorial works*, like so:

Rainbows
Rainbows–Pictorial works

6. I am cataloging a work on the professional ethics of librarians in East Germany, when it was the German Democratic Republic. Find the *SHM* rule and section that will help me determine what to assign for the geographic aspect of this work, and then pick which subject heading string below is correct according to the *SHM* instructions:

Librarians–Professional ethics–Germany
ANSWER: Incorrect. According to *SHM* H 0945 (Germany) section 1, use *–Germany (East)* for works discussing the German Democratic Republic from 1949 to 1990.

Librarians–Professional ethics–Germany (East)
ANSWER: Correct. According to *SHM* H 0945 (Germany) section 1, use *–Germany (East)* for works discussing the German Democratic Republic from 1949 to 1990.

Librarians–Professional ethics–Germany (Democratic Republic, 1949-)
ANSWER: Incorrect. According to *SHM* H 0945 (Germany) section 1, use *–Germany (East)* for works discussing the German Democratic Republic from 1949 to 1990.

CHAPTER 7

1. A work about krump dancing in Toronto, Canada. **ANSWER:**

   Krumping–Ontario–Toronto
   In MARC:
   650_0 $a Krumping $z Ontario $z Toronto

2. A directory of dog parks in Seattle, Washington. **ANSWER:**

   Parks for dogs–Washington (State)–Seattle–Directories
   In MARC:
   650 _0 $a Parks for dogs $z Washington (State) $z Seattle $v Directories

3. A periodical about employees in the sugar industry in Tokyo, Japan. **ANSWER:**

   Sugar trade–Japan–Tokyo–Employees–Periodicals
   In MARC:
   650 _0 $a Sugar trade $z Japan $z Tokyo $x Employees $v Periodicals

Sugar trade—Employees cannot be subdivided geographically, but *Sugar trade* can be subdivided geographically.

4. A work on the study and teaching of hippotherapy in the United States. **ANSWER:**

   Horsemanship–Therapeutic use–Study and teaching–United States
   In MARC:
   650 _0 $a Horsemanship $x Therapeutic use $x Study and teaching $z United States

5. A travel guidebook for Rome, Italy. **ANSWER:**

   Rome (Italy)–Guidebooks
   In MARC:
   651 _0 $a Rome (Italy) $v Guidebooks

6. A work on the effect of inflation on life insurance in Santa Fe, New Mexico. **ANSWER:**

   Life insurance–Effect of inflation on–New Mexico–Santa Fe
   In MARC:
   650_0 $a Life insurance $x Effect of inflation on $z New Mexico $z Santa Fe

7. A work about the evaluation of elementary schools in Minneapolis, Minnesota. **ANSWER:**

   Elementary schools–Minnesota–Minneapolis–Evaluation
   In MARC:
   650 _0 $a Elementary schools $z Minnesota $z Minneapolis $x Evaluation

–Evaluation cannot be subdivided geographically, so that is why it is at the end of the string.

8. A work on politics in Lisbon, Portugal, during the seventeenth century. **ANSWER:**

   Lisbon (Portugal)–Politics and government–17th century
   In MARC:
   651 _0 $a Lisbon (Portugal) $x Politics and government $y 17th century

9. A fiction work aimed at juveniles about collecting Hot Wheels toy cars in Canada. **ANSWER:**

   Hot Wheels toys–Collectors and collecting–Canada–Juvenile fiction
   In MARC:
   650 _0 $a Hot Wheels toys $x Collectors and collecting $z Canada $v Juvenile fiction

10. A work that consists of statistics on the reliability of rainfall in Rio de Janeiro, Brazil. **ANSWER:**

    Rainfall reliability–Brazil–Rio de Janeiro–Statistics
    In MARC:
    650 _0 $a Rainfall reliability $z Brazil $z Rio de Janeiro $v Statistics

11. A work on playing the children's game Chutes and Ladders in India. **ANSWER:**

    Leela (Game)
    In MARC:
    650 _0 $a Leela (Game)

This subject heading cannot be subdivided geographically, so do not include *–India*. And yeah, *Leela (Game)* for Chutes and Ladders?

12. A work on artificial satellites orbiting the planet Mars. **ANSWER:**

    Artificial satellites–Mars (Planet)
    or
    Artificial satellites–Mars (Planet)–Orbits
    In MARC:
    650 _0 $a Artificial satellites $z Mars (Planet)
    or
    650 _0 $a Artificial satellites $z Mars (Planet) $x Orbits

The authority record for *Mars (Planet)* says, "This heading is not valid for use as a geographic subdivision, except where specifically established."

Note the last part of the sentence: "except where specifically established." Looking in Classification Web, *Artificial satellites–Mars (Planet)* is there and is therefore "established" according to LC and means we can use *–Mars (Planet)* as a subdivision. LCSH for *Artificial satellites* further indicates that "works on artificial satellites of other celestial bodies are entered under Artificial satellites subdivided by the name of the body, e.g. Artificial satellites—Sun." *Orbits*, though not in the Free-Floating Subdivision list, is in Classification Web after *Artificial satellites–Mars (Planet)* and can be included as a topical subdivision if the "orbiting" aspect in the work is emphasized.

CHAPTER 8

1. List the authorized access point for each of the following using LC Authorities. If using MARC in your answer, include the coding that would be appropriate if the person is a subject heading in a bibliographic record (in other words, use the MARC 600 field):

    a. Tennis professional, Serena Williams. **ANSWER:**

Williams, Serena, 1981-
In MARC:
600 10 $a Williams, Serena, $d 1981-

   b. Author of the *Lord of the Rings*, J. R. R. Tolkien. **ANSWER:**

Tolkien, J. R. R. (John Ronald Reuel), 1892-1973
In MARC:
600 10 $a Tolkien, J. R. R. $q (John Ronald Reuel), $d 1892-1973

   c. Former president of the United States Ulysses S. Grant. **ANSWER:**

Grant, Ulysses S. (Ulysses Simpson), 1822-1885
In MARC:
600 10 $a Grant, Ulysses S. $q (Ulysses Simpson), $d 1822-1885

d. Ancient queen of Egypt Cleopatra. **ANSWER:**

Cleopatra, Queen of Egypt, -30 B.C.
In MARC:
600 00 $a Cleopatra, $c Queen of Egypt, $d -30 B.C.

2. Label each of the following as either the authorized access point or a variant access point for the heading for American music artist and producer Sean Combs, otherwise known as P. Diddy:
   a. Combs, Sean, 1969-. **ANSWER:** variant access point
   b. Puffy, 1969-. **ANSWER:** variant access point
   c. Diddy, 1969-. **ANSWER:** authorized access point
   d. Combs, Diddy, 1969-. **ANSWER:** variant access point
   e. P. Diddy, 1969-. **ANSWER:** variant access point

3. For each of the following works, assign the appropriate personal name subject heading and a Free-Floating Subdivision to convey the subject of this work. Consult *SHM* H 1110 (Free-Floating Subdivisions: Names of Persons) to find a suitable subdivision. You may also want to consult the Free-Floating Subdivisions list in Classification Web or search for them on the LC Authorities website.
   a. A work specifically about the assassination of American President Abraham Lincoln. **ANSWER:**

Lincoln, Abraham, 1809-1865–Assassination
In MARC:
600 10 $a Lincoln, Abraham, $d 1809-1865 $x Assassination

   b. A book of quotations by Irish poet and playwright Oscar Wilde. **ANSWER:**

Wilde, Oscar, 1854-1900–Quotations
In MARC:
600 10 $a Wilde, Oscar, $d 1854-1900 $v Quotations

c. Transcripts of interviews with American entertainer, singer, and model RuPaul. **ANSWER:**

RuPaul, 1960- –Interviews
In MARC:
600 00 $a RuPaul, $d 1960- $v Interviews

d. A juvenile fiction work that specifically focuses on Malcolm X's wife Betty Shabazz's early life. **ANSWER:**

Shabazz, Betty–Childhood and youth–Juvenile fiction
In MARC:
600 10 $a Shabazz, Betty $x Childhood and youth $v Juvenile fiction

e. A book about American poet Emily Dickinson's close friends. **ANSWER:**

Dickinson, Emily, 1830-1886–Friends and associates
In MARC:
600 10 $a Dickinson, Emily, $d 1830-1886 $x Friends and associates

4. For each of the following works, assign the appropriate personal name subject heading and at least one "class of persons" heading. You may also provide more specific "class of persons" headings if you deem them appropriate.
   a. A biography of Hispanic American film actor Ramon Novarro that emphasizes his Hispanic American ethnicity. **ANSWER:**

   Novarro, Ramon, 1899-1968
   Motion picture actors and actresses–United States–Biography
   Hispanic American motion picture actors and actresses–United States–Biography
   In MARC:
   600 10 $a Novarro, Ramon, $d 1899-1968
   650 _0 $a Motion picture actors and actresses $z United States $v Biography

650 _0 $a Hispanic American motion picture actors and actresses $z United States $v Biography

 b. An autobiography of basketball player Yao Ming, who played the sport in both China and the United States. **ANSWER:**

Yao, Ming, 1980-
Basketball players–China–Biography
Basketball players–United States–Biography
In MARC:
600 10 $a Yao, Ming, $d 1980-
650 _0 $a Basketball players $z China $v Biography
650 _0 $a Basketball players $z United States $v Biography

The biography form subdivision is still appropriate as *Autobiography* is a UF term according to LCSH. Include two fields for *Basketball players* to capture his participation in basketball in the United States and China.

 c. A memoir written by and about journalist and television producer Janet Mock that emphasizes her transgender identity and racially mixed heritage. **ANSWER:**

Mock, Janet, 1983-
Racially mixed people–United States–Biography
Transgender women–United States–Biography
In MARC:
600 10 $a Mock, Janet, $d 1983-
650 _0 $a Racially mixed people $z United States $v Biography
650 _0 $a Transgender women $z United States $v Biography

If you included occupational categories such as *Women journalists–United States–Biography* or *Women television producers and directors–United States–Biography*, that is fine too. You may have also thought to include *African American women journalists–United States–Biography* or *African American women in television broadcasting–United States–Biography*, and while these would not be altogether inaccurate, they obviously overlook the mixed-race aspect of her identity. This is a subjective decision that comes down to what extent her occupation is discussed in the work.

  d. A biography of American boxer Muhammad Ali for a juvenile audience (the fact that he is African American is not a significant aspect of this work). **ANSWER:**

Ali, Muhammad, 1942-2016–Juvenile literature
Boxers (Sports)–United States–Biography–Juvenile literature
In MARC:
600 10 $a Ali, Muhammad, $d 1942-2016 $v Juvenile literature
650 _0 $a Boxers (Sports) $z United States $v Biography $v Juvenile literature

The fact that he is African American is not a significant aspect of this work, so do not add another field for African American boxers.

CHAPTER 9

1. Using LCSH (not CSH), determine if *–Fiction* or *–Juvenile fiction* is most appropriate as a form subdivision for subject headings applied to fiction works aimed at each of the following target audiences:
   a. First graders. **ANSWER:** *–Juvenile fiction*
   b. High school seniors. **ANSWER:** *–Juvenile fiction*
   c. Seventh graders. **ANSWER:** *–Juvenile fiction*
   d. College freshmen. **ANSWER:** *–Fiction*
2. For each of the form headings below, use *SHM* H 1790 to determine if a topical heading is needed when cataloging a fiction collection by one or more authors:
   a. Short stories. **ANSWER:** Yes—this form heading is broad and nontopical.
   b. Erotic stories. **ANSWER:** No—this form heading is specific and contains a topical aspect.
   c. Science fiction, Canadian. **ANSWER:** No—this form heading contains topical and national aspects.

d. Bildungsromans. **ANSWER:** No—this form heading is specific.
   e. Diary fiction. **ANSWER:** Yes—this form heading is broad and nontopical.
   f. Beat fiction. **ANSWER:** No—this form heading is specific and contains a topical aspect.
3. In which MARC field should form headings be encoded? **ANSWER:** 655
4. According to *SHM* H 1790, section 4, which of the following headings should be applied to individual works of fiction?
   a. Form headings
   b. Topical headings that express the biographical aspects of the work
   c. Topical headings that express the psychological aspects of the work
   d. Topical headings that express the historical aspects of the work

ANSWER: b and d

5. Which section of *SHM* H 1790 was added in 2001 that encouraged LC catalogers to increase subject access to works of fiction? What works of fiction are included in its scope? Which categories of headings may be appropriate to apply to works covered in this section? **ANSWER:**

Special Provisions for Increased Subject Access to Fiction; Individual works of fiction; Form/genre, character, setting, topic

6. Identify and correct the errors in the cataloging for individual works of fiction assigned the headings in each of the following scenarios:
   a. A fantastical retelling of the life of Chinese philosopher Confucius. **ANSWER:**

Confucius (does not have –Fiction subdivision)
Fantasy fiction

b. A romance between two electricians. **ANSWER:**

Electricians–Fiction
Fiction (Violates the rule of specificity; should be removed)
Romance fiction

c. A mystery that involves two office employees, a man and a woman, who work together. **ANSWER:**

Man-woman relationships–Fiction (Violates the suggestion to avoid vague and general topics [e.g., interpersonal relationships]; should be removed)
Clerks–Fiction
Detective and mystery stories

d. A contemporary novel about scientists in Zimbabwe written by a Namibian author in English. **ANSWER:**

Scientists–Zimbabwe–Fiction
Namibian fiction (English)–21st century (Chronological subdivision should be removed since the book was written in this century)

7. In the remaining exercises, assign Library of Congress subject headings and subdivisions as well as genre/form headings (if needed) to the works described below. Use Classification Web (or another source for finding LCSH if you cannot access Classification Web), the Library of Congress Authorities website (http://authorities.loc.gov/) or another authority file, the *Guidelines on Subject Access to Individual Works of Fiction, Drama, Etc.*, and/or *Library of Congress Genre/Form Terms for Library and Archival Materials*. If you prefer, encode your answers in MARC.
a. A juvenile fiction work on the extinction of dinosaurs. **ANSWER:**

Dinosaurs–Extinction–Juvenile fiction
In MARC:
650 _0 $a Dinosaurs $x Extinction $v Juvenile fiction

b. A collection of environmental fiction short stories. **ANSWER:**

Ecofiction
In MARC:
655 _0 $a Ecofiction
or
655 _7 $a Ecofiction. $2 lcgft

This heading is in both LCSH and *LCGFT*.

c. A collection of fiction by various Swedish authors, primarily about European football and fans of the sport (use a broad, non-topical form heading). **ANSWER:**

Soccer–Fiction
Soccer fans–Fiction
Swedish fiction
In MARC:
650 _0 $a Soccer $v Fiction
650 _0 $a Soccer fans $v Fiction
655 _0 $a Swedish fiction

d. A choose-your-own-story novel (for a juvenile audience) about animal robots and children who are inventors. **ANSWER:**

Robotic animals–Juvenile fiction
Children as inventors–Juvenile fiction
Plot-your-own stories (in LCSH)
Choose-your-own stories (in LCGFT)
In MARC:
650 _0 $a Robotic animals $v Juvenile fiction
650 _0 $a Children as inventors $v Juvenile fiction
655 _0 $a Plot-your-own stories
655 _7 $a Choose-your-own stories. $2 lcgft

e. A fiction book within the "steampunk" genre that features a cursed amulet and romance. **ANSWER:**

Cursed objects–Fiction
Amulets–Fiction
Steampunk fiction
Romance fiction
In MARC:
650 _0 $a Cursed objects $v Fiction
650 _0 $a Amulets $v Fiction
655 _0 $a Steampunk fiction
655 _0 $a Romance fiction

Steampunk fiction and *Romance fiction* are in *LCGFT* as well. Therefore, you could have this instead of the LCSH form/genre answers:

655 _7 $a Steampunk fiction. $2 lcgft
655 _7 $a Romance fiction. $2 lcgft

You could also have *Love stories* from *GSAFD*:

655 _7 $a Love stories. $2 gsafd

Appendix B
Form and Topical Free-Floating Subdivisions

The following free-floating subdivisions are from the *Subject Headings Manual* (*SHM*) H 1095, Free-Floating Subdivisions. They are free-floating subdivisions of general application. Additional free-floating subdivisions are available and discussed in other *SHM* instructions, such as H 1110, Names of Persons, and H 1140, Names of Places (both of which are listed in the next two appendices). I recommend using this list as a way to familiarize yourself with the breadth of free-floating subdivisions available, but consult Classification Web or *SHM* H 1095 to confirm their defined scope before assigning them. In addition to including a scope note for each subdivision, each entry in *SHM* H 1095 also references other *SHM* instructions that relate to the subdivision. For example, *SHM* H 1206.5 (Acronyms) is referenced in the $x Acronyms entry.

MARC subfield codes are included ($x = topical subdivision and $v = form subdivision), and keep in mind that some form subdivisions can be used as a topical subdivision if a resource is *about* the form. If you do not need to use MARC coding, then ignore the $x's and $v's at the beginning of each subdivision.

$x Abbreviations
$x Abbreviations $v Dictionaries
$v Abbreviations of titles
$x Ability testing (May Subd Geog)
$x Abstracting and indexing (May Subd Geog)

$v Abstracts
$x Access control (May Subd Geog)
$x Accidents (May Subd Geog)
$x Accidents $x Investigation (May Subd Geog)
$x Accounting
$x Accreditation (May Subd Geog)
$x Acronyms
$x Acronyms $v Dictionaries
$x Administration
$v Aerial photographs
$x Air conditioning (May Subd Geog)
$x Air conditioning $x Control (May Subd Geog)
$v Amateurs' manuals
$x Analysis
$v Anecdotes
$x Anniversaries, etc.
$x Archival resources
$v Archives
$x Archives $v Microform catalogs
$v Art
$v Atlases
$x Audio-visual aids
$x Audio-visual aids $v Catalogs
$v Audiocassette catalogs
$v Audiotape catalogs
$x Auditing
$x Authorship
$x Authorship $v Style manuals
$x Automatic control
$x Automation
$x Autonomous communities
$x Autonomous regions
$x Awards (May Subd Geog)
$x Barrier-free design (May Subd Geog)
$x Biblical teaching
$v Bibliography
$v Bibliography $v Catalogs

$v Bibliography $v Early
$v Bibliography $v Exhibitions
$x Bibliography $x Methodology
$v Bibliography $v Microform catalogs
$v Bibliography $v Union lists
$v Bibliography of bibliographies
$v Bio-bibliography
$v Bio-bibliography $v Dictionaries
$v Biography
$v Biography $v Dictionaries
$v Biography $v Dictionaries $x French [Italian, etc.]
$x Biography $x History and criticism
$v Blogs
$v Book reviews
$x Buildings
$v By-laws
$x By-products
$v Calendars
$x Calibration
$x Cantons
$v Caricatures and cartoons
$v Case studies
$v Catalogs
$v Catalogs and collections (May Subd Geog)
$v CD-ROM catalogs
$x Censorship (May Subd Geog)
$x Centennial celebrations, etc.
$x Certification (May Subd Geog)
$x Charitable contributions (May Subd Geog)
$v Charts, diagrams, etc.
$v Chronology
$x Circulation
$x Citizen participation
$v Classification
$x Cleaning (May Subd Geog)
$v Code numbers
$v Code words

$x Cold weather conditions
$x Collectibles (May Subd Geog)
$x Collection and preservation (May Subd Geog)
$x Collectors and collecting (May Subd Geog)
$x Colonies
$v Comic books, strips, etc.
$x Communication systems
$v Compact disc catalogs
$x Comparative method
$v Comparative studies
$x Competitions (May Subd Geog)
$x Composition
$x Computer-aided design (May Subd Geog)
$x Computer-assisted instruction
$v Computer games
$x Computer network resources
$x Computer networks (May Subd Geog)
$x Computer networks $x Security measures (May Subd Geog)
$x Computer programs
$x Computer simulation
$v Concordances
$v Congresses
$x Congresses $x Attendance
$x Conservation and restoration (May Subd Geog)
$x Control (May Subd Geog)
$v Conversion tables
$x Cooling (May Subd Geog)
$x Corrosion (May Subd Geog)
$x Corrupt practices (May Subd Geog)
$x Cost control
$x Cost effectiveness
$x Cost of operation
$x Costs
$v Cross-cultural studies
$x Cult (May Subd Geog)
$x Curricula (May Subd Geog)
$x Customer services (May Subd Geog)

$x Data processing
$v Data tape catalogs
$v Databases
$x Dating
$x Decision making
$x Defects (May Subd Geog)
$x Defects $x Reporting (May Subd Geog)
$x Defense measures (May Subd Geog)
$x Departments
$x Design
$x Design and construction
$v Designs and plans
$x Deterioration (May Subd Geog)
$v Dictionaries
$v Dictionaries $x French [Italian, etc.]
$v Dictionaries $x Polyglot
$v Dictionaries, Juvenile
$x Digitization (May Subd Geog)
$v Directories
$x Discipline
$v Discography
$x Documentation (May Subd Geog)
$v Drama
$v Drawings
$x Drying (May Subd Geog)
$x Dust control (May Subd Geog)
$v Early works to 1800
$x Earthquake effects (May Subd Geog)
$x Econometric models
$x Economic aspects (May Subd Geog)
$x Electromechanical analogies
$v Electronic discussion groups
$x Electronic information resources
$x Electronic publishing (May Subd Geog)
$x Employees
$v Encyclopedias
$v Encyclopedias, Juvenile

$x Endowments
$x Energy conservation (May Subd Geog)
$x Energy consumption (May Subd Geog)
$x Environmental aspects (May Subd Geog)
$x Equipment and supplies
$x Estimates (May Subd Geog)
$x Evaluation
$x Examinations
$x Examinations $v Study guides
$v Examinations, questions, etc.
$v Excerpts
$v Exhibitions
$x Experiments
$x Expertising (May Subd Geog)
$v Facsimiles
$v Fiction
$x Fieldwork (May Subd Geog)
$v Film catalogs
$x Finance
$x Fires and fire prevention (May Subd Geog)
$v Folklore
$x Food service (May Subd Geog)
$x Forecasting
$z Foreign countries
$x Foreign influences
$x Forgeries (May Subd Geog)
$v Forms
$v Formulae, receipts, prescriptions
$x Fuel systems
$x Fume control (May Subd Geog)
$x Geographic information systems (May Subd Geog)
$x Government policy (May Subd Geog)
$x Governorates
$x Grading (May Subd Geog)
$x Graphic methods
$v Guidebooks
$v Handbooks, manuals, etc.

$x Health aspects (May Subd Geog)
$x Heating and ventilation (May Subd Geog)
$x Heating and ventilation $x Control (May Subd Geog)
$x Heraldry
$x Historiography
$x History
$x History $y To 1500
$x History $y 16th century
$x History $y 17th century
$x History $y 18th century
$x History $y 19th century
$x History $y 20th century
$x History $y 21st century
$x History $v Chronology
$x History $x Philosophy
$x History $v Sources
$x History and criticism
$x History of doctrines
$x History of doctrines $y Early church, ca. 30-600
$x History of doctrines $y Middle Ages, 600-1500
$x History of doctrines $y 16th century
$x History of doctrines $y 17th century
$x History of doctrines $y 18th century
$x History of doctrines $y 19th century
$x History of doctrines $y 20th century
$x History of doctrines $y 21st century
$x Hot weather conditions (May Subd Geog)
$v Humor
$x Hurricane effects (May Subd Geog)
$x Identification
$v Illustrations
$v In art
$x In literature
$x In mass media
$x In motion pictures
$x In opera
$v Indexes

$x Industrial applications (May Subd Geog)
$x Influence
$x Information resources
$x Information resources management (May Subd Geog)
$x Information services
$x Information technology (May Subd Geog)
$x Insignia
$x Inspection (May Subd Geog)
$x Installation (May Subd Geog)
$x Instruments
$v Interactive multimedia
$x International cooperation
$x Internet marketing (May Subd Geog)
$x Interpretation
$v Inventories
$x Inventory control (May Subd Geog)
$v Job descriptions (May Subd Geog)
$v Juvenile drama
$v Juvenile fiction
$v Juvenile films
$v Juvenile humor
$v Juvenile literature
$v Juvenile poetry
$v Juvenile software
$v Juvenile sound recordings
$x Labeling (May Subd Geog)
$x Labor productivity (May Subd Geog)
$v Laboratory manuals
$x Landscape architecture (May Subd Geog)
$x Language
$v Legends
$x Library resources
$x Licenses (May Subd Geog)
$x Licenses $x Fees (May Subd Geog)
$x Lighting (May Subd Geog)
$x Linear programming
$v Literary collections

$x Liturgy
$x Liturgy $v Texts
$x Location (May Subd Geog)
$v Longitudinal studies
$x Maintenance and repair
$x Management
$x Manuscripts
$x Manuscripts $v Catalogs
$v Manuscripts $v Facsimiles
$x Manuscripts $v Indexes
$x Manuscripts $v Microform catalogs
$v Maps
$x Maps $v Bibliography
$v Maps $v Early works to 1800
$v Maps $v Facsimiles
$x Maps $x Symbols
$x Marketing
$x Materials (May Subd Geog)
$x Mathematical models
$x Mathematics
$x Measurement
$x Medals (May Subd Geog)
$x Medical examinations (May Subd Geog)
$v Meditations
$x Membership
$x Methodology
$v Microform catalogs
$v Miscellanea
$x Models (May Subd Geog)
$x Moisture (May Subd Geog)
$x Moral and ethical aspects (May Subd Geog)
$x Museums (May Subd Geog)
$x Mythology (May Subd Geog)
$x Name
$x Names
$v Newspapers
$x Noise

$v Nomenclature
$v Nomograms
$v Notation
$v Observations
$v Observers' manuals
$x Officials and employees
$x On postage stamps
$x On television
$v Online chat groups
$x Orbit
$v Outlines, syllabi, etc.
$x Packaging (May Subd Geog)
$x Packing (May Subd Geog)
$v Pamphlets
$v Papal documents
$v Parodies, imitations, etc.
$v Passenger lists
$v Patents
$v Periodicals
$x Periodicals $v Abbreviations of titles
$x Periodicals $v Bibliography
$x Periodicals $v Bibliography $v Catalogs
$x Periodicals $v Bibliography $v Union lists
$x Periodicals $v Indexes
$v Personal narratives
$x Personal narratives $x History and criticism
$x Personnel management
$x Philosophy
$v Photographs
$v Photographs from space
$x Physiological aspects
$x Physiological effect (May Subd Geog)
$v Pictorial works
$x Planning
$v Poetry
$x Political activity (May Subd Geog)
$x Political aspects (May Subd Geog)

$v Popular works
$v Posters
$x Power supply (May Subd Geog)
$x Practice (May Subd Geog)
$v Prayers and devotions
$x Prayers and devotions $x History and criticism
$x Preservation (May Subd Geog)
$x Press coverage (May Subd Geog)
$x Prevention
$x Prices (May Subd Geog)
$x Prices $x Government policy (May Subd Geog)
$x Private collections (May Subd Geog)
$v Problems, exercises, etc.
$x Production and direction (May Subd Geog)
$x Production control (May Subd Geog)
$x Production standards (May Subd Geog)
$v Programmed instruction
$x Programming (May Subd Geog)
$x Prophecies
$x Protection (May Subd Geog)
$x Provinces
$x Psychological aspects
$x Psychology
$x Public opinion
$x Public relations (May Subd Geog)
$x Publishing (May Subd Geog)
$x Purchasing (May Subd Geog)
$x Quality control
$v Quotations, maxims, etc.
$x Qur'anic teaching
$x Rates (May Subd Geog)
$v Readings with music
$v Records and correspondence
$x Recreational use (May Subd Geog)
$x Reference books
$x Regional disparities
$x Regions

$v Registers
$x Reliability
$x Remodeling (May Subd Geog)
$x Remodeling for other use (May Subd Geog)
$x Remote sensing
$x Repairing (May Subd Geog)
$x Republics
$x Research (May Subd Geog)
$x Research grants (May Subd Geog)
$v Reviews
$x Risk assessment (May Subd Geog)
$v Romances
$v Rules
$v Rules and practice
$x Safety appliances (May Subd Geog)
$x Safety measures
$x Safety regulations (May Subd Geog)
$x Sanitation (May Subd Geog)
$x Scholarships, fellowships, etc. (May Subd Geog)
$x Scientific applications (May Subd Geog)
$x Security measures (May Subd Geog)
$v Sermons
$x Sermons $x History and criticism
$x Sex differences (May Subd Geog)
$x Signers
$x Simulation games
$x Simulation methods
$x Slang
$v Slides
$x Social aspects (May Subd Geog)
$x Societies, etc.
$x Sociological aspects
$v Software
$v Songs and music
$x Songs and music $v Discography
$x Songs and music $x History and criticism
$v Songs and music $v Texts

$x Soundproofing (May Subd Geog)
$v Sources
$v Specifications (May Subd Geog)
$x Spectra
$v Speeches in Congress
$x Stability
$x Standards (May Subd Geog)
$x State supervision (May Subd Geog)
$x States
$x Statistical methods
$x Statistical services
$v Statistics
$x Storage (May Subd Geog)
$x Study and teaching (May Subd Geog)
$x Study and teaching $x Activity programs (May Subd Geog)
$x Study and teaching $x Audio-visual aids
$x Study and teaching $x Simulation methods
$x Study and teaching $x Supervision (May Subd Geog)
$x Study and teaching (Continuing education) (May Subd Geog)
$x Study and teaching (Continuing education) $x Audio-visual aids
$x Study and teaching (Early childhood) (May Subd Geog)
$x Study and teaching (Early childhood) $x Activity programs (May Subd Geog)
$x Study and teaching (Early childhood) $x Audio-visual aids
$x Study and teaching (Elementary) (May Subd Geog)
$x Study and teaching (Elementary) $x Activity programs (May Subd Geog)
$x Study and teaching (Elementary) $x Audio-visual aids
$x Study and teaching (Elementary) $x Simulation methods
$x Study and teaching (Graduate) (May Subd Geog)
$x Study and teaching (Higher) (May Subd Geog)
$x Study and teaching (Higher) $x Activity programs (May Subd Geog)
$x Study and teaching (Higher) $x Audio-visual aids
$x Study and teaching (Higher) $x Simulation methods
$x Study and teaching (Internship) (May Subd Geog)
$x Study and teaching (Middle school) (May Subd Geog)

$x Study and teaching (Middle school) $x Activity programs (May Subd Geog)
$x Study and teaching (Middle school) $x Audio-visual aids
$x Study and teaching (Preschool) (May Subd Geog)
$x Study and teaching (Preschool) $x Activity programs (May Subd Geog)
$x Study and teaching (Preschool) $x Audio-visual aids
$x Study and teaching (Primary) (May Subd Geog)
$x Study and teaching (Primary) $x Activity programs (May Subd Geog)
$x Study and teaching (Primary) $x Audio-visual aids
$x Study and teaching (Residency) (May Subd Geog)
$x Study and teaching (Secondary) (May Subd Geog)
$x Study and teaching (Secondary) $x Activity programs (May Subd Geog)
$x Study and teaching (Secondary) $x Audio-visual aids
$x Study and teaching (Secondary) $x Simulation methods
$v Study guides
$v Tables
$v Tables of contents
$x Taxation (May Subd Geog)
$x Taxation $x Law and legislation (May Subd Geog)
$x Technique
$x Technological innovations (May Subd Geog)
$v Telephone directories
$v Terminology
$x Terminology $x Pronunciation
$x Territories and possessions
$x Testing
$v Textbooks
$v Texts
$x Themes, motives
$x Therapeutic use (May Subd Geog)
$x Tombs (May Subd Geog)
$x Toxicology (May Subd Geog)
$v Trademarks
$x Translating (May Subd Geog)

$v Translations
$v Translations into [name of language]
$x Transportation (May Subd Geog)
$x Tropical conditions
$v Union lists
$x Union territories
$v Use studies
$x Validity (May Subd Geog)
$x Valuation (May Subd Geog)
$x Vibration (May Subd Geog)
$x Vocational guidance (May Subd Geog)
$x Voivodeships
$x Waste disposal (May Subd Geog)
$x Waste minimization (May Subd Geog)
$x Water-supply
$x Web-based instruction (May Subd Geog)
$x Weight
$x Weights and measures

Appendix C
Names of Places in Free-Floating Subdivisions

The following free-floating subdivisions are from the *Subject Headings Manual* (*SHM*) H 1140, Names of Places. They are free-floating subdivisions that can be assigned to names of geographic places as established in a name authority file (such as the Library of Congress Authorities website: http://authorities.loc.gov/). Refer to chapter 7, "Geographic Subject Headings and Subdivisions," of this book for further discussion of geographic places as subjects.

Many of these subdivisions cannot be assigned to or are restricted to specific types of geographic places. For example, *–Antiquities* should not be placed after names of extinct cities and *–Eruptions* should be assigned only to names of volcanoes. Consult Classification Web or *SHM* H 1140 to confirm a subdivision's defined scope before assigning it.

MARC subfield codes are included ($x = topical subdivision and $v = form subdivision), and keep in mind that some form subdivisions can be used as a topical subdivision if a resource is *about* the form. If you do not need to use MARC coding, then ignore the $x's and $v's at the beginning of each subdivision. Note how most *cannot* be subdivided geographically.

$x Abstracting and indexing (May Subd Geog)
$v Abstracts
$x Administrative and political divisions
$x Aerial exploration
$v Aerial film and video footage

$v Aerial photographs
$v Aerial views
$x Altitudes
$v Anecdotes
$x Annexation to [. . .]
$x Anniversaries, etc.
$x Antiquities
$x Antiquities $x Collection and preservation (May Subd Geog)
$x Antiquities $x Collectors and collecting (May Subd Geog)
$x Antiquities, Byzantine
$x Antiquities, Celtic
$x Antiquities, Germanic
$x Antiquities, Phoenician
$x Antiquities, Roman
$x Antiquities, Slavic
$x Antiquities, Turkish
$x Appropriations and expenditures
$x Appropriations and expenditures $x Effect of inflation on
$x Archival resources
$x Area
$x Armed Forces (May Subd Geog)
$v Audiocassette catalogs
$v Audiotape catalogs
$v Bio-bibliography
$v Biography
$v Biography $v Anecdotes
$v Biography $v Caricatures and cartoons
$v Biography $v Dictionaries
$v Biography $v Dictionaries $x French [Italian, etc.]
$x Biography $x History and criticism
$v Biography $v Humor
$v Biography $v Pictorial works
$v Biography $v Portraits
$x Biography $v Sources
$v Book reviews
$x Boundaries (May Subd Geog)
$x Buildings, structures, etc.

$x Buildings, structures, etc.–Conservation and restoration
$v Calendars
$x Capital and capitol
$v Census
$x Census $x Law and legislation
$v Census, [date]
$x Centennial celebrations, etc.
$v Charters
$v Charters, grants, privileges
$x Church history
$x Church history $y 16th century
$x Church history $y 17th century
$x Church history $y 18th century
$x Church history $y 19th century
$x Church history $y 20th century
$x Church history $y 21st century
$x Civilization
$x Civilization $y 16th century
$x Civilization $y 17th century
$x Civilization $y 18th century
$x Civilization $y 19th century
$x Civilization $y 20th century
$x Civilization $y 21st century
$x Civilization $x Foreign influences
$x Civilization $x Philosophy
$x Claims
$x Claims vs. . . .
$x Climate
$x Climate $v Observations
$x Colonial influence
$x Colonies
$x Colonization
$x Commerce (May Subd Geog)
$x Commercial policy
$v Commercial treaties
$v Compact disc catalogs
$x Court and courtiers

$x Court and courtiers $x Clothing
$x Court and courtiers $x Food
$x Court and courtiers $x Language
$x Cultural policy
$x Defenses
$x Defenses $x Economic aspects
$x Defenses $x Law and legislation
$x Dependency on [place]
$x Dependency on foreign countries
$x Description and travel
$v Directories
$x Discovery and exploration
$x Discovery and exploration $x French [Spanish, etc.]
$x Distances, etc.
$v Drama
$v Early works to 1800
$x Economic conditions
$x Economic conditions $y 16th century
$x Economic conditions $y 17th century
$x Economic conditions $y 18th century
$x Economic conditions $y 19th century
$x Economic conditions $y 20th century
$x Economic conditions $y 21st century
$x Economic conditions $y [period subdivision] $x Regional disparities
$x Economic conditions $x Regional disparities
$x Economic integration
$x Economic policy
$x Emigration and immigration
$x Emigration and immigration $x Economic aspects
$x Emigration and immigration $x Government policy
$x Emigration and immigration $x Religious aspects
$x Emigration and immigration $x Social aspects
$x Environmental conditions
$x Environmental conditions $y 16th century
$x Environmental conditions $y 17th century
$x Environmental conditions $y 18th century
$x Environmental conditions $y 19th century

$x Environmental conditions $y 20th century
$x Environmental conditions $y 21st century
$x Eruption, [date]
$x Eruptions
$x Ethnic relations
$x Ethnic relations $x Economic aspects
$x Ethnic relations $x Political aspects
$v Fiction
$v Folklore
$x Forecasting
$x Foreign economic relations (May Subd Geog)
$x Foreign public opinion
$x Foreign public opinion, Austrian [British, etc.]
$x Foreign relations (May Subd Geog)
$x Foreign relations $x Catholic Church
$x Foreign relations $v Executive agreements
$x Foreign relations $x Law and legislation
$x Foreign relations $x Philosophy
$x Foreign relations $v Treaties
$x Foreign relations administration
$v Gazetteers
$v Genealogy
$x Genealogy $x Religious aspects
$x Geography
$x Gold discoveries
$v Guidebooks
$x Historical geography
$x Historical geography $v Maps
$x Historiography
$x History
$x History $y 16th century
$x History $y 17th century
$x History $y 18th century
$x History $y 19th century
$x History $y 20th century
$x History $y 21st century
$x History $y [period subdivision] $v Biography

$x History $y [period subdivision] $v Biography $v Anecdotes
$x History $y [period subdivision] $v Biography $v Portraits
$x History $y [period subdivision] $x Biography $v Sources
$x History $y [period subdivision] $v Chronology
$x History $y [period subdivision] $x Historiography
$x History $y [period subdivision] $x Philosophy
$x History $y [period subdivision] $v Sources
$x History $v Anecdotes
$x History $x Autonomy and independence movements
$x History $v Chronology
$x History $v Comic books, strips, etc.
$x History $x Errors, inventions, etc.
$x History $v Humor
$x History $x Periodization
$x History $x Philosophy
$x History $v Pictorial works
$x History $x Prophecies
$x History $x Religious aspects
$x History $v Sources
$x History, Local
$x History, Local $x Collectibles
$x History, Military
$x History, Military $y 16th century
$x History, Military $y 17th century
$x History, Military $y 18th century
$x History, Military $y 19th century
$x History, Military $y 20th century
$x History, Military $y 21st century
$x History, Military $x Religious aspects
$x History, Naval
$x History, Naval $y 16th century
$x History, Naval $y 17th century
$x History, Naval $y 18th century
$x History, Naval $y 19th century
$x History, Naval $y 20th century
$x History, Naval $y 21st century
$v Humor

$v Imprints
$v In art
$x In bookplates
$x In literature
$x In mass media
$x In motion pictures
$x In opera
$x In popular culture
$x Information services
$x Intellectual life
$x Intellectual life $y 16th century
$x Intellectual life $y 17th century
$x Intellectual life $y 18th century
$x Intellectual life $y 19th century
$x Intellectual life $y 20th century
$x Intellectual life $y 21st century
$x International status
$v Juvenile drama
$v Juvenile fiction
$v Juvenile humor
$v Juvenile poetry
$x Kings and rulers
$x Kings and rulers $x Abdication
$x Kings and rulers $x Art patronage
$x Kings and rulers $x Assassination
$x Kings and rulers $x Brothers
$x Kings and rulers $x Children
$x Kings and rulers $x Death and burial
$x Kings and rulers $x Deposition
$x Kings and rulers $x Dwellings
$x Kings and rulers $x Education
$x Kings and rulers $v Folklore
$x Kings and rulers $v Genealogy
$x Kings and rulers $x Heraldry
$x Kings and rulers $x Mythology
$x Kings and rulers $x Paramours
$x Kings and rulers $x Religious aspects

$x Kings and rulers $x Sisters
$x Kings and rulers $x Succession
$x Kings and rulers $x Tombs
$x Kings and rulers $x Travel (May Subd Geog)
$x Languages
$x Languages $x Law and legislation
$x Languages $x Political aspects
$x Languages $v Texts
$x Library resources
$v Literary collections
$v Literatures
$v Maps
$x Maps $v Bibliography
$v Maps $v Early works to 1800
$v Maps $v Facsimiles
$x Military policy
$x Military policy $x Religious aspects
$x Military relations (May Subd Geog)
$x Militia
$x Moral conditions
$x Name
$x National Guard
$x Naval militia
$v Newspapers
$x Officials and employees (May Subd Geog)
$x Officials and employees $x Accidents (May Subd Geog)
$x Officials and employees $z Foreign countries
$x Officials and employees $z Foreign countries $x Foreign language competency
$x Officials and employees $x Furloughs
$x Officials and employees $x Leave regulations
$x Officials and employees $x Payroll deductions
$x Officials and employees $x Salaries, etc. (May Subd Geog)
$x Officials and employees $x Salaries, etc. $x Regional disparities
$x Officials and employees $x Turnover
$x Officials and employees, Alien
$x Officials and employees, Honorary

$x Officials and employees, Retired
$x On postage stamps
$x On television
$v Photographs from space
$v Pictorial works
$v Poetry
$x Politics and government
$x Politics and government $y 16th century
$x Politics and government $y 17th century
$x Politics and government $y 18th century
$x Politics and government $y 19th century
$x Politics and government $y 20th century
$x Politics and government $y 21st century
$x Politics and government $y [period subdivision] $x Philosophy
$x Politics and government $x Philosophy
$x Population
$x Population $x Economic aspects
$x Population $x Environmental aspects
$x Population policy
$v Posters
$x Press coverage (May Subd Geog)
$v Quotations, maxims, etc.
$x Race relations
$x Race relations $x Economic aspects
$x Race relations $x Political aspects
$v Registers
$x Relations (May Subd Geog)
$v Relief models
$x Religion
$x Religion $y 16th century
$x Religion $y 17th century
$x Religion $y 18th century
$x Religion $y 19th century
$x Religion $y 20th century
$x Religion $y 21st century
$x Religion $x Economic aspects
$x Religious life and customs

$v Remote-sensing images
$x Research (May Subd Geog)
$x Rural conditions
$x Scheduled tribes
$x Seal
$v Slides
$x Social conditions
$x Social conditions $y 16th century
$x Social conditions $y 17th century
$x Social conditions $y 18th century
$x Social conditions $y 19th century
$x Social conditions $y 20th century
$x Social conditions $y 21st century
$x Social life and customs
$x Social life and customs $y 16th century
$x Social life and customs $y 17th century
$x Social life and customs $y 18th century
$x Social life and customs $y 19th century
$x Social life and customs $y 20th century
$x Social life and customs $y 21st century
$x Social policy
$v Songs and music
$x Songs and music $x History and criticism
$v Songs and music $v Texts
$x Statistical services
$x Statistical services $x Law and legislation
$v Statistics
$v Statistics, Medical
$v Statistics, Vital
$x Strategic aspects
$x Study and teaching (May Subd Geog)
$x Study and teaching $x Law and legislation (May Subd Geog)
$v Surveys
$x Symbolic representation
$v Telephone directories
$v Telephone directories $v Yellow pages
$x Territorial expansion

$x Territories and possessions
$x Territories and possessions $x Politics and government
$v Tours
$v Trials, litigation, etc.

Appendix D
Names of Persons in Free-Floating Subdivisions

The following free-floating subdivisions are from the *Subject Headings Manual* (*SHM*) H 1110, Names of Persons. They are free-floating subdivisions that can be assigned to names of persons as established in a name authority file (such as the Library of Congress Authorities website: http://authorities.loc.gov/). Consult Classification Web or *SHM* H 1110 to confirm their defined scope before assigning them.

According to *SHM* H 1110, personal name headings include "all personal names established in the name authority file except for names of non-human entities (e.g., names of individual fictitious and legendary characters, individual gods and mythological figures, and individually named animals)," as outlined by the Library of Congress in Free-Floating Subdivisions: Names of Persons—H 1110 (*Subject Headings Manual*, last modified August 2020, https://www.loc.gov/aba/publications/FreeSHM/H1110.pdf). Refer to chapter 8, "Personal Name Subject Headings and Biographies," of this book for further discussion of personal names as subjects.

MARC subfield codes are included ($x = topical subdivision and $v = form subdivision), and keep in mind that some form subdivisions can be used as a topical subdivision if a resource is *about* the form. If you do not need to use MARC coding, then ignore the $x's and $v's at the beginning of each subdivision. Note how most *cannot* be subdivided geographically.

$x Abdication
$v Abstracts

$v Adaptations
$x Adversaries
$x Aesthetics
$x Alcohol use
$x Allusions
$v Anecdotes
$x Anniversaries, etc.
$x Anonyms and pseudonyms
$x Appreciation (May Subd Geog)
$x Archaeological collections
$v Archives
$v Art
$x Art collections
$x Art patronage
$x Assassination
$x Assassination attempts
$v Audio adaptations
$v Audiocassette catalogs
$v Audiotape catalogs
$x Authorship
$x Authorship $x Collaboration
$v Autographs
$x Awards
$v Bibliography
$x Birth
$x Birthplace
$v Blogs
$x Bonsai collections
$x Books and reading
$v Calendars
$x Captivity
$v Caricatures and cartoons
$v Catalogs
$v Catalogues raisonnés
$x Censorship (May Subd Geog)
$x Censures
$x Characters

$x Childhood and youth
$v Chronology
$x Cipher
$x Claims vs. . . .
$x Clothing
$x Coin collections
$x Comedies
$v Comic books, strips, etc.
$v Compact disc catalogs
$v Concordances
$x Contemporaries
$x Coronation
$v Correspondence
$x Correspondence $v Microform catalogs
$x Criticism, Textual
$x Criticism and interpretation
$x Criticism and interpretation $x History
$x Criticism and interpretation $x History $y To 1500
$x Criticism and interpretation $x History $y 16th century
$x Criticism and interpretation $x History $y 17th century
$x Criticism and interpretation $x History $y 18th century
$x Criticism and interpretation $x History $y 19th century
$x Criticism and interpretation $x History $y 20th century
$x Criticism and interpretation $x History $y 21st century
$x Cult (May Subd Geog)
$x Death and burial
$x Death mask
$v Diaries
$x Disciples
$v Discography
$x Divorce
$v Drama
$x Dramatic production
$x Dramatic works
$x Dramaturgy
$x Drug use
$x Employees

$x Estate
$x Ethics
$x Ethnological collections
$x Ethnomusicological collections
$x Examinations
$v Examinations, questions, etc.
$x Exile (May Subd Geog)
$x Family
$v Fiction
$x Fictional works
$v Film adaptations
$x Finance, Personal
$x First editions
$x First editions $v Bibliography
$x Forgeries (May Subd Geog)
$x Freemasonry
$x Friends and associates
$x Hadith
$x Harmony
$x Health
$x Herbarium
$x Homes and haunts (May Subd Geog)
$v Humor
$v Illustrations
$x Impeachment
$x Imprisonment
$x In bookplates
$x In literature
$x In mass media
$x In motion pictures
$x In opera
$x Inauguration
$x Influence
$x Information services
$v Interviews
$v Juvenile drama
$v Juvenile fiction

$v Juvenile humor
$v Juvenile poetry
$x Kidnapping
$x Knowledge and learning
$x Language
$x Language $v Glossaries, etc.
$x Last years
$v Legends
$x Library $v Marginal notes
$x Library $v Microform catalogs
$x Library resources
$v Literary collections
$x Literary style
$x Manuscripts
$v Manuscripts $v Facsimiles
$x Map collections
$x Marriage
$x Medals
$v Meditations
$x Mental health
$x Military leadership
$x Miracles
$x Monuments (May Subd Geog)
$x Motion picture plays
$x Museums (May Subd Geog)
$x Musical instrument collections
$v Musical settings
$x Musical settings $x History and criticism
$x Name
$x Natural history collections
$v Notebooks, sketchbooks, etc.
$x Numismatic collections
$x Numismatics
$x On postage stamps
$x On television
$x Oratory
$v Outlines, syllabi, etc.

$x Palaces (May Subd Geog)
$x Pardon
$v Parodies, imitations, etc.
$x Performances (May Subd Geog)
$x Philosophy
$x Photograph collections
$v Pictorial works
$x Poetic works
$v Poetry
$x Political activity (May Subd Geog)
$x Political and social views
$v Portraits
$x Poster collections
$v Posters
$v Prayers and devotions
$x Prayers and devotions $x History and criticism
$x Pre-existence
$x Prophecies
$x Prose
$x Psychology
$x Public opinion
$v Quotations
$x Radio and television plays
$x Relations with men
$x Relations with women
$x Relics (May Subd Geog)
$x Religion
$x Resignation from office
$v Romances
$v Scholia
$x Scientific apparatus collections
$x Seal
$v Self-portraits
$v Sermons
$x Settings
$x Sexual behavior
$x Shrines (May Subd Geog)

$x Slide collections
$v Slides
$x Societies, etc.
$v Songs and music
$x Songs and music $x History and criticism
$v Songs and music $v Texts
$v Sources
$x Spiritualistic interpretations
$v Spurious and doubtful works
$x Stage history (May Subd Geog)
$x Stamp collections
$x Statues (May Subd Geog)
$v Stories, plots, etc.
$x Symbolism
$x Teachings
$x Technique
$v Telephone calls
$v Television adaptations
$v Thematic catalogs
$x Themes, motives
$x Titles
$x Tomb
$x Tragedies
$x Tragicomedies
$v Translations
$x Translations $x History and criticism
$v Translations into French [German, etc.]
$x Translations into French [German, etc.] $x History and criticism
$x Travel (May Subd Geog)
$v Trials, litigation, etc.
$x Versification
$x Will
$x Writing skill
$x Written works

Glossary

associative relationship: A relationship between two related terms or concepts that is not hierarchical or equivalent.

authority records: Records that document information about a specific agent (e.g., person, corporate body, family), title (e.g., work, series), or subject.

authorized access point: "A standardized access point representing an entity."[1]

chronological subdivision: A subdivision that conveys time period.

controlled vocabulary: A standardized list of terms, or "headings," that is used to describe something. Ideally, controlled vocabulary terms are *unique* (only one heading represents a particular topic) and are applied *consistently* so that all works on a particular topic can be found under one term. Controlled vocabularies often contain variant terms associated with the "authorized" terms.

equivalence relationship: A relationship of two or more terms that are considered synonymous within a controlled vocabulary, with one term chosen as the "authorized" one.

form subdivision: A subdivision that conveys what a resource *is* as opposed to what it is *about*.

free-floating subdivisions: Primarily topical and form subdivisions that can be used with main subject headings within a particular scope, regardless of whether or not the subdivisions appear in the main LCSH list.

geographic subdivision: A subdivision that conveys a geographic location.

hierarchical relationship: Arranging terms in relation to one another from broader to more specific within a particular context.

literary warrant: The idea that the inclusion of a subject heading or subdivision in a controlled vocabulary is determined largely by its presence in published literature.

Machine-Readable Cataloging (MARC): A commonly used standard for encoding bibliographic data in library catalogs. The MARC syntax includes three-digit field codes that designate the general meaning of each field, two indicators that have a different meaning depending on the field, and subfields that begin with a delimiter symbol and a lowercase letter or number. Though there are multiple MARC standards, the most common ones are bibliographic and authority MARC.

main headings: Terms that describe what a work is primarily about.

pattern headings: designated headings within specific topic areas that are followed by free-floating subdivisions appropriate to that topic area within LCSH.

postcoordination: Occurs when terms are combined by those searching the system, such as in a keyword search.

precoordination: Occurs when terms are combined within the controlled vocabulary itself or by someone assigning the vocabulary term(s) to create a complex topic. In other words, precoordinated terms representing a topic are determined prior to a user's search of a system.

scope-match: "The level of depth at which books are indexed."[2]

specificity: Defined in two primary ways: (1) it refers to how closely the topic of a resource matches the term(s) applied; and (2) it refers to the lowest part of a hierarchy within a particular context.

subdivisions: Terms that add further specificity to main headings, such as a time period, geographic place, or other topics, if needed.

subject analysis: The process of determining what a resource is about and, to a lesser degree, its form and/or genre.

subject heading string: A string of subjects that consists of one main subject heading and one or more subdivisions.

topical subdivision: A subdivision that conveys a concept or object.

variant access point: "An alternative to an authorized access point representing an entity."[3]

NOTES

1. RDA Steering Committee, "Authorized Access Point," RDA Toolkit, last modified April 2017, http://access.rdatoolkit.org/.

2. Library of Congress, "Doing Research at the Library of Congress: Three Basic Principles of Library of Congress Subject Headings," last modified December 1, 2016, https://www.loc.gov/rr/main/research/scopematch.html.

3. RDA Steering Committee, "Variant Access Point," RDA Toolkit, last modified April 2017, http://access.rdatoolkit.org/.

Index

20 percent rule, 7, 49, 87, 89

aboutness. *See* subject analysis
associative relationships, 4–6
authority files, 40–41, 60, 70, 86, 102
authority records, 8, 41, 60–62, 66, 69, 70, 102
authorized access point, viii, 40, 42, 61–62, 66, 69, 71, 73, 77

biographical works, subject headings and subdivisions for, ix, 69, 71–77
broader term (BT), 21–22, 34, 52

Cataloging Lab, 51, 103
Children's and Young Adults' Cataloging (CYAC) program, 96–97
children's materials. *See* juvenile materials
chronological subdivisions. *See* subdivisions
Classification Web, ix, 7, 17, 19–27, 32–35, 38, 94, 96, 102
conceptual analysis. *See* subject analysis

controlled vocabulary, vii–viii, 1, 3, 12, 14–17

ethical issues, 1–2, 88
equivalence relationships, 3–4

fiction works, subject headings and subdivisions for, ix, 81–100
form/genre headings, 40, 46–47, 82–87, 93–95
form headings. *See* form/genre headings
form subdivisions. *See* subdivisions
free-floating subdivisions. *See* subdivisions

genre headings. *See* form/genre headings
geographic subdivisions. *See* subdivisions
geographic subject headings, ix, 45, 55, 59–63, 66, 77, 89–90
GSAFD. *See* Guidelines on Subject Access to Individual Works of Fiction, Drama, Etc.

Guidelines on Subject Access to Individual Works of Fiction, Drama, Etc. (GSAFD), 93–95, 102

hierarchical relationships, 4–5

juvenile materials, subject headings and subdivisions for, 13, 16, 50, 81–83, 87, 95–97

LCGFT. *See* Libindexrary of Congress Genre/Form Terms for Library and Archival Materials.
Library of Congress, vii, 1, 7, 49, 83, 88
Library of Congress Children's Subject Headings, 7, 13, 81, 95–97, 102
Library of Congress Genre/Form Terms for Library and Archival Materials (LCGFT), 7, 40, 46–47, 93–95, 102
literary warrant, 1

Machine-Readable Cataloging (MARC), ix, 25, 35, 37–47, 61–63, 70, 73, 85, 94, 97, 103
main headings, 2, 22, 31, 39, 51
MARC. *See* Machine-Readable Cataloging

narrower term (NT), 21–22, 34, 52

pattern headings, 53–54
personal name subject headings, ix, 40–42, 66, 69–79, 91–92
precoordination, 16–17
postcoordination, 16–17

Resource Description & Access (RDA), 60, 70
related term (RT), 21–22

scope-match, 6–7, 89
scope notes, 33–35, 63, 72
see also (SA), 21–22
SHM. *See* Subject Headings Manual
SLAM method, 8, 12–15, 17
specificity, 3, 6, 51, 89
subdivisions, ix, 3, 22, 29, 31–35, 39, 42, 44–46, 53–54
  chronological, 30, 33, 40, 44–45, 75–76, 89–90, 95
  form, 30, 32–33, 39, 44–45, 73
  free-floating, 32–34, 53–54, 62, 71–72, 76, 81
  geographic, ix, 22, 30–33, 44, 40, 44–45, 55, 63–66, 77, 89–90, 95
  topical, 29, 32–34, 40, 42–45
subject analysis, ix, 11–17
  aboutness, 12–14
  conceptual analysis, 12
  translation, 12, 15
subject heading string, 29, 34
Subject Headings Manual (SHM), ix, 2, 6–8, 29, 31, 33, 35, 44–45, 47, 49–57, 59–60, 62–65, 72–77, 83–91, 93–94, 97, 102

topical subdivisions. *See* subdivisions
topical subject headings, 2, 34, 38–39, 44–45, 51, 65, 73, 77, 84–89
translation. *See* subject analysis

used for (UF), 21–22, 34
use (Use), 21–22

variant access point, viii, 3, 61–62, 70

About the Author

Karen Snow is an associate professor and the PhD program director in the School of Information Studies at Dominican University in River Forest, Illinois. She teaches face-to-face and online in the areas of cataloging, classification, and metadata. She completed her PhD in information science at the University of North Texas in 2011 while working as a cataloger in the rare book rooms of the university archives and the technical services departments. Her main areas of research interest are cataloging quality, ethics, and education. In 2016, she received the Follett Corporation's Excellence in Teaching Award. Her first book, *A Practical Guide to Library of Congress Classification*, was published by Rowman & Littlefield in 2017.

www.ingramcontent.com/pod-product-compliance
Lightning Source LLC
Chambersburg PA
CBHW022014300426
44117CB00005B/176